STORIES OF A LIFE

STORIES
OF A LIFE

Some Startling,
Some Funny,
Always Fascinating

CARL MILLER

SUNSTONE
PRESS

SANTA FE

NOTE: Events, dates, and opinions current as of the date of the
publication of this book.

Sunstone books may be purchased for educational, business, or sales promotional use.
For information please write: Special Markets Department, Sunstone Press,
P.O. Box 2321, Santa Fe, New Mexico 87504-2321.

Book and cover design › Vicki Ahl
Body typeface › ITC Benguiat
Printed on acid-free paper
∞
eBook 978-1-61139-558-7

———————————

Library of Congress Cataloging-in-Publication Data

On File

———————————

WWW.SUNSTONEPRESS.COM
SUNSTONE PRESS / POST OFFICE BOX 2321 / SANTA FE, NM 87504-2321 /USA
(505) 988-4418 / ORDERS ONLY (800) 243-5644 / FAX (505) 988-1025

Dedication

To all the people who were and are a part of this story, and especially to my wife Sandra Thomas who had encouraged me to write this book for many years. Also to Cindy Fry who made so many of the connections.

Contents

2 / Early Influences   / 47

3 / Peace Corps in South America, 1963–1965   / 59

4 / Japan / 101

5 / Back Surgery / 109

6 / Santa Fe, New Mexico / 111

7 Writing Books / 151

Epilogue / 159

Preface

This is not a conventional memoir, but rather what the title says: stories of a life. I've elected to give the reader a look at my many experiences that were wide ranging and diverse, The stories are broken into the major events, loosely chronological, but mostly just "stand alones" that focus on one subject or activity that I have found most significant and enjoyable...and even important to share, perhaps.

I've also included some photographs that have meant a lot to me. You'll have to forgive the poor quality of most of them, but they are what they are and they reflect the atmosphere of the times.

I hope you enjoy reading my book as much as I've enjoyed writing it—and living what I wrote about.

1

My Family

Paternal Grandparents

My grandmother Clara and her future husband first met when they were children in 1901 at Ellis Island. Her family came from Switzerland and his from Germany. Their families first settled in New York and both their parents moved to southern Indiana within a couple of years and then to Chicago. Later on when they were in their early thirties, they married and made their home in Chicago. They had two children: my father Jerry and his sister Virginia.

My grandfather went to work for a trucking company. He died at the age of thirty-eight on the road just outside Chicago when an infected gallbladder burst. My dad used to brag that my grandfather was 6'5" and weighed 250 pounds. My grandmother would challenge that and say he was 6'1" and weighed 215. Splitting hairs I guess. My dad and grandmother agreed, though, that my grandfather had a 48" chest, a 35" waist, and a 25" thigh.

Clara was a petite, attractive woman, about 5'3" and 110 pounds. She had dark hair and blue eyes. She was a caring person—very positive and active. After her husband died four men proposed to her, but sadly each one died suddenly three to four weeks before they were to be married. The last one was accidentally electrocuted using some machinery right in front of her while they were panning for gold in the Mohave desert. She loved panning for gold and did it almost every weekend. Clara supported herself and her children in real estate when they lived in Chicago and after moving to the Los Angeles area in the 1940s.

Clara died in 1982 of cancer. She loved her rose bushes and the morning before she died, I called to see how she was doing. She said that she was just enjoying the rose bushes outside her window.

Growing up mostly in the San Fernando Valley my two cousins, children of my mother's brother, and I had many chances to hop a vegetable train from the fields in Van Nuys to Ventura. We played Batman and Robin inside and outside the train and we'd come back at night to continue. We met many people along the way and they were very friendly and got a kick out of what we were doing. We exchanged stories over the summers. Some of these people were migrant workers, some were young teenagers, and some were residents of the San Fernando Valley. We all got along well. This was near my grandmother Clara's home and I went over and enjoyed her quiet company when we would take walks and talk. Much later in life, after my dad died, I would spend several weeks with her.

Aunt Virginia

My father's sister Virginia was two years his elder. She was blonde, petite, striking, outgoing and a stylish dresser. Virginia lived most of the time with my grandmother and was very caring toward her. Besides dating Al Capone, yes Al Capone, she dated lots of Italian men but she never married. Both my father and Aunt Virginia attended Northwestern University in Evanston, Illinois, but it was expensive so she dropped out and went to work for a clothing store. She did really well and was able to afford all the top brands.

As she told it, Al Capone took a liking to her because of her style of dressing. He escorted her to many clubs and introduced her to his friends. At one point Al was responsible for a killing and he left Chicago for the summer, taking my aunt with him. According to her, they both enjoyed northern Michigan. Coming back to Chicago in the fall, she said the heat on Al had blown over. But it wasn't long before she broke off that relationship and went back to living with her mother and sometimes he brother Jerry (my father). Later she was living with her mother until she died of stomach cancer just a couple of years before my father Jerry died.

My Mother and Her Parents

My mom, Elizabeth McRae, was raised in Pittsburgh along with a brother and sister. Her father was superintendent of schools and an avid golfer and bowler. Unfortunately, her mother was admitted to a psychiatric asylum in her early forties and died there. My grandfather visited her every weekend and was heartbroken both when she had to be admitted to the asylum and when she died.

When my grandfather retired he made a lot of trips to see his son and my mother in the Los Angeles area and to Kansas to see his other daughter. In his late eighties he was still golfing and bowling in the 110s. He taught me how to play chess, which I later taught to my younger son Kyle.

My mother Elizabeth was tall, dark haired and elegant. She was the first cigarette girl for a major tobacco company. She studied in Chicago to get her nursing degree and went back many times for more nursing courses. She was very good at it and had an excellent bedside manner, resulting in a long career as a nurse and she really enjoyed it. Starting as a surgical nurse she later worked for a dermatologist who did hair transplants for stars like Frank Sinatra and Joey Bishop. This was a new procedure at the time and a very bloody one at that. When she was older she enjoyed getting out and doing ear piercings in department stores. Unfortunately, she could never stop smoking and died of emphysema at the age of seventy-nine. Even though she was a nurse, she would say, "They have never proven that cigarette smoking caused lung disease." When she was in the hospital dying, her last request was for a cigarette.

My mother met my father, Jerry Miller, at the 1932 Olympic swimming tryouts. She was a swimmer like my dad. They both tried out for the 100 meter freestyle but neither made the Olympic team, which went to Holland. I believe the tryouts were held in Chicago. Although my father went on to compete in water polo, my mother gave up competitive swimming and concentrated on her nursing education.

Drinking and parties were a part of their lives and they both imbibed with relish. Dancing was also a part of that scene.

I remember Mom keeping an immaculate house, even though she always had cats, and she kept her beloved Oriental furniture polished. She was a big supporter of my sister Kathy and me. She chauffeured Kathy around to dance lessons and performances and cheerleading. Besides supporting me in school, she was an enthusiastic backer of my athletic activities, later embarrassing my stepfather by walking up and down the sidelines during my football games cheering me on. She also attended my track meets.

I was so busy with school and sports that I didn't have time to read, but my mother loaned me two of her books anyway. When I went to college I was asked what I had read. I remembered one of the titles she had loaned me: *Too Much Too Soon* by Diana Barrymore—pretty racy book for the time. She always pushed me to be the best and really wanted me to become a doctor. She was insistent on this and I finally told her I had a doctor's degree: "Doctor of Advice, Better when not taken." She finally accepted the fact that I was not going to go into medicine, although I tried, so she pushed me to be the best in whatever I did. Later in life she continued to support me when I ran for political office.

Nevertheless, when I was thirty-six years old and well into a teaching and coaching career, I applied and was accepted to the University of New Mexico Medical School. This was after the death of my father, detailed later in this book, and I thought at the time that he had left me sufficient money to pay for it. However, the committee that oversaw the money decided that the wording of the will did not allow for coverage of my education. (It did, however, cover the education of my two sons.) I disagreed with the committee's interpretation since the will said I could use the money for health and education. The lawyer handling my dad's monies was on board for maybe three months at the most. We had three meetings when I stopped in Chicago on my way back from the Olympics in Montreal, Canada. My grandmother, who received monies, told me she would have gone to bat for me if she had been five to ten years younger. She said she loved me very much and was sure I should get a share, but she didn't have the energy to go to court. So I did not go to medical school. I go into this again later.

As I was writing this book, I found that I began to remember a lot more about my past that has shaped me. I remember that off and on I would be afraid of being alone. At one time when my mom lived at the Royal Palms Hotel across from MacArthur Park in Los Angeles and when I was about four or five, she started dating my stepfather (more about this later) and she would leave me by myself at the hotel when they went out—no babysitter or relatives. This left me with the feeling of being alone and insecure as I went through the course of my life. Once I traced this feeling back to those times, I was better able to adjust to a feeling of being abandoned. Maybe those early experiences accounted for my being late for some functions. My mother even said I would be late for her funeral. But I wasn't!

My Father

My dad Jerry Miller used to sleep on the fire escape in Chicago when he was a young man (maybe 19 to 22 years old) so my grandmother and his sister Virginia could be by themselves. I'm sure the weather might have dictated when that was feasible. It was always hot in the summer and very cold in the winter.

As I said earlier, both my father and Aunt Virginia attended Northwestern University. It was expensive and when my Aunt Virginia dropped out, my dad got to stay because of a swimming and water polo scholarship. But he needed money for himself, his sister and his mother. Previously he had been a professional boxer so he got back into the sport. He had said he was good but not great and the money he earned boxing barely covered the expenses of his family. He really learned racial discrimination there and unfortunately came to hate almost all the ethnic groups by boxing against them and experiencing their behavior toward him and each other.

This went on for several years and my dad said it was a pleasure to have done it for his family. In his fourth year at Northwestern his sister moved to Taluca Lake in the San Fernando Valley, a region of Los Angeles County, and moved in with my grandmother. My grandmother's real estate business had taken off and Aunt Virginia with her clothing background began modeling and made a good living.

My father graduated from Northwestern in political science and education. My mother, as I've said, was an excellent swimmer and their interest in swimming was a bind that eventually led to marriage and my being born in February of 1940.

Marines, World War II, South Pacific

My father enlisted in the Marine Corps in 1942, hoping to use his swimming skills which he did. Because of his swimming ability he was assigned to underwater demolition. His job was to place explosives on the hulls of Japanese ships and managed to sink six ships. He got to see much of the Pacific war and was actively involved in some of it on the islands. Here he developed a negative opinion of the Japanese at that time because of the brutality they showed against their prisoners as well as the native people of the islands they had occupied. My dad ended the war guarding Japanese POW in Tianjin, China.

Water Polo and the Olympics, 1936, 1948

My father made many significant decisions in his life that had an effect on me. Before the war he did what I consider a very bright thing. When he was at Northwestern he tried out for the 100 freestyle, but he found out he didn't have the blazing speed it required. He wanted to go the 1936 Olympic Games in Berlin. He had tried out for the 1932 100 meter free style but didn't make it. It occurred to him that since he was fast enough, he thought about what other physical talents he had. Well, he thought, I have very good hand to eye coordination, so he took up water polo and trained hard at Northwestern University and the Chicago Athletic Club.

His goal to make the 1936 Olympic Games turned out and the USA water polo team placed fourth. As much as he had loved playing water polo at those 1936 Olympic Games in Berlin he was sorry that they were held in Berlin because he felt this gave status to the German Nazis and that Hitler used it as a propaganda machine. He wished the games had been elsewhere.

During World War II there were no Olympic Games in 1940 and 1944.

After the war my dad qualified for the 1948 Olympic Games held in London. Again the USA Water Polo Team came in fourth. As an aside, on the ship on the way over to London there were many sports doctors taking various measurements on the athletes. No drinking was allowed. The top female swimmer was caught with one drink and sent home.

My dad had been smoking and drinking since he was twelve but had a tremendous physical constitution. The only other athlete I met who did the same thing was a University of California guard on the National Collegiate Basketball Championship. I roomed in the same house with him and saw him do that regularly.

Through the years, my dad kept smoking and drinking, but he also kept swimming. When his liver got bad, he'd stop until it was okay and then he'd go back to his old habits.

Divorce

When my dad came back from the Pacific he surprised us all by divorcing my mother Elizabeth and moving to Chicago. I then had to balance two families. Fortunately both my parents remarried people with colorful personalities and one was wonderful. (More later.) My mom was in Los Angeles and married Lenard Kenith McRae who had been badly wounded in this right knee by the Germans in the Normandy invasion. My dad married a socialite from Ohio, Marilyn Miller. The court battles over my custody raged between Dad in Chicago and Mom in Los Angeles for two years. Finally, after a bitter battle, he was granted summer custody of me and at the age of nine I started spending the summers with him in Chicago. One of the reasons he fought for me was that his new wife Marilyn couldn't have children. I later learned that my dad had actually married Marilyn before divorcing my mother, so she could have put him in jail.

My dad always told me to write to my mother when I was with him, but on the other hand my mother hated my dad so much she couldn't have cared less whether or not I wrote to him when I was with her.

When I was with my dad in the summers we would go out to dinner with Marilyn and their friends. He always wanted me to speak up and enter into the table talk. Many times I had nothing to say and he would reprimand me for this. In many of my interactions with people I would not say anything or maybe just a few words if I actually had to. Much of my life was made up of situations where I had little or nothing to say. I worked on ways to solve this problem and eventually developed ways to do so.

His Way or Nothing

Over time my dad would reward me with things if I let him have his way. Here are some examples where we did not see things the same way:

In high school I saved up enough money to buy my mom and stepdad's 1947 Pontiac. It sure got me around. I drove all over the San Fernando Valley and even Los Angeles. In the two years I had it, I had six fender benders—all my fault! Backing up was hard for me and still is today. What I really wanted was a 1952 MG. Pop (my stepdad) loaned me a thousand dollars to buy it. My dad wouldn't loan me the money because it wasn't his choice of car. He wanted me to buy a Cadillac. This was in part how he treated me."You want something, do it my way and it's yours. If not, then nothing."

Once when I wanted to open up a vitamin store he said "no." At the time, I believed strongly in vitamin supplementation, but he did not.

At another time I told him that I wanted to run for political office (more on this later) and he commented that where I wanted to run was a district of 6-1 democratic and heavily Hispanic. To overcome the odds in such a district, I would have to quit my teaching job at the time and go door to door. He said he would support me financially, but he didn't. He gave me no support of any kind and I lost the election. It was a real shame because I came within four points of winning. My stepmother Marilyn had said, "Jerry let him do what he wants to do and you back him up." It was very hard for him to do this because what he actually wanted me to do was go into the insurance business with him.

Insurance Agency

After the war he wanted to make a lot of money. His majors at Northwestern didn't prepare him for anything that would bring in big money but he realized that the insurance field really challenged and interested him. In those days substandard insurance with pre-existing conditions was hard to get. So he worked hard and got great underwriters in the Midwest. He set up his insurance agency at 208 S. LaSalle in Chicago. He played "the game" and worked to be successful, even if it meant cheating. For example, if he thought an insurer's urine sample would not be acceptable to an insurance company, he would dump it, fill the bottle with his own good urine and send it in. But he was always very generous to his office staff. They received generous salaries and bonuses and increased insurance coverage.

Working with Dad in the Insurance Business

I ended up working two summers for him and he said I did a great job. And people I had come in contact with also said they thought I had a great future in insurance. But I really hated it. I felt it was a boring and a low class profession, akin to selling encyclopedias.

During the those summers we took long vacations to Canada. My dad was not only fond of these vacations but also the two Indian guides we had with us each time, Two and Longmont. From the border of Canada we would take a train eighty-eight miles to Lake Wabatongushi and our guides would meet us there when we got off the train. We stayed in a cabin and caught lots of walleye and pike. We ate and drank in a dining hall and Dad drank heavily each night, but he was always up and ready to go the next morning.

Later, when my dad died, I found out that he was called "Big Jake" by people in the newspaper business and on the radio and TV. I had never heard of him referred to that way and this led me to suspect that my dad was into a lot of things I knew nothing about. I did know about his plan to expand his business into Los Angeles and that he was in negotiations with Franklin Roosevelt's son Jimmy to head up and run the Los Angeles office. This opened my eyes as to the way many businesses are run: you go where the money is. In this case, Jimmy Roosevelt had many connections and ways to make money. His left of center politics was of no concern to my right of center dad, however.

Swimming

Dad always believed it was good to stay in shape so at lunchtime he would walk over to the Chicago Athletic Club and swim a mile and a half daily. He firmly believed that the swimming cleared his mind. Even in his early sixties he would swim two miles to my one mile, but he abused his body by smoking several packs of cigarettes a day and continued to drink a lot. He was convinced that he could do this if he kept exercising. I couldn't believe how much energy he had. He would wake up at six or seven in the morning and have a big breakfast to start the day. I knew only one other athlete who could play at a top level and smoke and drink excessively—and that was the guard I mentioned earlier at the University of California national basketball team.

At night when the weather was good we played badminton on our grass. I couldn't beat him until he was fifty-five. I beat everyone else but it took a long time to beat him.

Slugging the Police and Eddie Barrett

Dad was supportive when I took up Olympic lifting and coaching, and he always told me that no one gives a damn about second place. First is the only place that counts. But that was a lot of hot air, because there were many times when I didn't win and he was very proud of me anyway.

But he could be mean. Once, coming into Chicago from a vacation, a police car stopped him for speeding. My dad jumped out of the car and said, "Do you know who I am? I am Jerry Miller." The policeman replied, "I don't care how you are. You were speeding." My dad said, "If you give me a ticket, I'll report you to Eddie Barrett, the District Attorney." The policeman just kept writing up the ticket and suddenly my dad slugged him and knocked him down and said after getting his number that he would report him to Eddie Barrett and he did. But Eddie Barrett said, "Jerry, I can't do anything about the policeman just doing his job," and then my dad knocked him down also. He then told Barrett that if he did anything about this incident he would report him to Mayor Daly. I was shocked by this behavior and realized that I would never use the "higher ups" to help me out of such a situation.

Al Capone

When my dad was at Northwestern University at a football game he once kicked Al Capone out of the stadium because he was drinking since drinking was not allowed in the stadium. A guy next to Al said, "Do you know who this is?" My dad replied, "I don't care if it is Al Capone." And the guy said, "Yes, he is Al Capone". But later on my dad played golf with Capone. At one time Capone put a golf ball on his chin, lay down and dared my dad to hit his golf ball from there. My dad said he was real scared, but he did it. Later that summer, Capone took a gun out of his golf bag and accidentally shot himself in the thigh. He was taken to the hospital and the whole floor was covered with Al's guards.

About a year later, Al was accused of first degree murder, which he said he didn't do. As I mentioned earlier, that was when he grabbed my Aunt Virginia and took her to upper Michigan where he hid out for the summer.

Through Capone my dad met several Mafia characters, like King Solomon, and he used them to protect him. I think he needed to protect himself and his family from people due to his insurance scams from time to time. One man I really remember was Dan Murphy. He protected me after my dad died and from King Solomon's son years. There will be more about that story later in this book!

His Reaction to the Peace Corps

Later on after I attended graduate school I was going to enlist in the military but at that time I had married my first wife Lynn Waterman and the military was not taking men who were married, so I applied to the Peace Corps. My dad hit the roof. We had gotten accepted to serve in Colombia and my dad said, "You could be making a lot of money for me, have private athletic facilities and you want to earn peanuts and go to some jungle?" When the FBI came to interview him about my Peace Corps application, my dad threw him out of the office. More on the Peace Corps later.

Car Crash and Marilyn's Death

Later on after living in Japan for three years, we planned to move to Santa Fe and this idea didn't go over well with much of my family. My dad said Santa Fe was very, very Democratic and my interest in going into politics would be fruitless and my interest in Olympic weight lifting would be the same. There was only one man in New Mexico, Clarence Bass of Albuquerque, who had done anything in Olympic weightlifting.

My wife Lynn at the time was born and raised in Santa Fe and I sensed that her going with me into the Peace Corps and to Japan was not really very appealing to her. Moving to Santa Fe and raising a family there would be more to her liking. So much later when we came back from Japan, we went to Chicago to visit my dad and stepmother Marilyn and to pick up a VW bus my father-in-law had gotten for us to drive to Santa Fe. He worked for Ford in Santa Fe and because of this, we got a good price. It was green and we called it the "Green Hornet." We planned to stay in Chicago for five or six days and just relax and have a good time.

On a Sunday while we were there my dad and I played golf at Bob-O-Link Golf Club, restricted to men. The men loved it as they could go around the golf course in whatever scanty clothes they wanted to and they could tell off-color stories. They mostly liked war stories as many of them had been in WWII and some in WWI. The Germans used a lot of gas in WWI and a lot of the golfers loved to hear stories involving the gas. Gas was outlawed in war, so it made the stories even more interesting. After a golf day we would go to the Hyatt Hotel for dinner.

That Sunday after dinner, my wife and I jumped in the "Green Hornet" and headed to Santa Fe. The next day around two in the afternoon the police managed to tracked us down somehow and told us that my dad and his wife Marilyn had been in a car accident and that Marilyn had died. We quickly turned around and went back to Chicago. In the hospital my dad was very banged up, with a lacerated face, broken nose and severed ear which had been re-attached. I knew he had memorized many phone numbers but I didn't realize how many until I was in the hospital with him. He called people for hours to let them know what had happened. In his conversations he repeated over and over that he believed in God but didn't like the way God voted.

His description of the accident was that a food truck had swiped him into the concrete overpass support. He said the crash had totaled the car and he kept saying that Marilyn's seat belt had cut her in half. He wasn't wearing a seat belt, so the crash sent him into the steering wheel and windshield. He swore he had not been drinking, but that was clearly false. They were going home from the golf club where we had left them and he was drunk. For days he kept on saying he blamed the food truck and if Marilyn's seat belt hadn't been on, she would be alive.

He was released from the hospital after a week and we had Marilyn's funeral. Following the funeral, I rode with Marilyn's body to Napoleon, Ohio, where she was born and raised and she was buried there. The doctor wouldn't let my dad go because of his injuries.

My wife took a plane to Santa Fe while I stayed in Chicago with my dad to help him through the emotional trauma. It was then that I had a spinal fusion of my lower back L-1-5 and sacrum. I had been having trouble with my back from a bull hitting me in Colombia three years prior. More on this later.

During the month in Chicago with my dad, I noticed a lot of his quirks. One day, for example, I was driving his Cadillac in town and he suddenly got mad at me and said, "You were to fight me when you turned sixteen. We never did it, so we will do it now." I was surprised at this outburst and got out of it by reminding him that my back had just been fused and the doctor said it would take six months to heal. Any sudden or other stressful motion before that would ruin the fusion—and it has been only ten days. I was scared, really scared because he could do it and would do it. I pleaded with him not to fight me and I pulled over to the side of the road and told him that if he wanted to go home, he was going to drive because I was not. I had seen him fly off the handle before, like the day he knocked out that policeman who was going to give him a ticket, as I mentioned before.

That whole month of my being with him reminded me of Christ on the cross, in such pain from taking on the total pains of the world. Because of Marilyn being killed in that car accident that might have been his fault, it seemed everything bad he had done in his life had come up to haunt him. I sincerely believed that this was enough of an example to keep me on the straight and narrow.

During the month I brought in many of his friends to help him—military (Marines) and business acquaintances. Each time he had a visitor, it only lasted about five to ten minutes before he asked the person to leave. Nothing would console him and he would stay awake many nights crying, moaning and yelling. When I left him at the end of the month, I didn't know if I would ever see him alive again.

When I got on the road to Santa Fe in the Green Hornet I couldn't help but notice how tin sounding it was. Boy did that ring true driving across Nebraska. I went there to meet Peary and Mabel Rader who owned Iron Man Industries. A part of their business was the publication of *Iron Man Magazine*. Through the years they gave Bob Hoffman's York Industries good competition. The three of us had a very productive time and formed a good rapport. I wrote for the magazine for many years until Rader's death.

I then continued on to Santa Fe where a job was waiting for me teaching sports and Russian history at Santa Fe Preparatory School.

Going Off the Deep End

Meanwhile over the next three years, my dad was very lonely, guilty, depressed, and agitated. In the Spring of 1971, he met Matt Hamlin, a national buyer for Carson Pirie Scott department stores. He chased her all over the country—she traveled a lot in her job—and sure enough, he convinced her to marry him.

In November, 1971 I went to Chicago to be the witness of their marriage. It was to take place in the office of Eddie Barrett, long-time Democratic Cook County Clerk. Eddie's wall looked like a who's who of the Illinois Democratic party and more from the 1920s on. I remember Eddie saying, "Jerry, you are a Republican but we have always worked well together." Meanwhile, Dad had told me, "If this doesn't work out, you will immediately get fifty thousand dollars. And I will get out of this with a pre-nuptial agreement." It turned out he never had one.

So the next day Eddie Barrett married my dad and Matt before Jack Falls, Bernie Lindquist, Matt Hickey, and myself. When it was done, my dad winked at me and said "Remember what I told you?" and flashed me the thumb and big finger rub indicating money.

It wasn't long after that, in the summer of 1972, that I started receiving calls from my dad stating that the marriage was not working out, that Matt just nagged him and nagged him. He reminded me of the pre-nuptial agreement and the fifty thousand I would get. "Eddie Barrett would take care of everything." Sure.

Before their wedding in 1971, my dad had stopped drinking. He had this game he'd play. Periodically the doctor would take a liver biopsy and if his liver was going bad he would stop drinking. Then, when his liver recuperated, he would start drinking again. Although his last liver test in 1971 was good, he stopped drinking anyway. One of the reasons he said he married Matt was that she got him to quit drinking and now she was drunk all the time. She often was drunk in bed or out getting something to eat and drink. She'd return home drunk and the doorman had to carry her up to the condo where they lived. He went over this time and again when I would go through Chicago and stay a day or two, having to travel when I became the United States World and Olympic weightlifting coach starting in the winter of 1974.

Once when I was returning from a coaches conference in Sofia, Bulgaria, I again stayed with him and he started in on a bizarre scenario as we drove away from the airport. He said he couldn't live with her, speaking of Matt. To divorce her would take half his money and he just couldn't stand that emotionally. I reminded him of the pre-nuptial agreement, and he mumbled something. I didn't question. He had said that she wouldn't be able to take care of herself with no money. This was certainly not true because she had made a lot of money in her previous job with Carson Pirie Scott. So he then intimated to my surprise that he was trying to kill her with arsenic and had been unsuccessful.

At the condo at 1 East Schiller in downtown Chicago, when Matt wasn't around, he showed me the arsenic. Then he laid out how he wanted me to come up the servant's elevator, which wasn't used much because he was in the penthouse on the eleventh floor, and mix the arsenic in with Matt's tea leaves in a jar in the cupboard. In theory, when she prepared her tea by spooning the tea leaves from the jar, the arsenic would be passed into her tea cup, and when she poured in the water, let the mixture steep, then drank it, the job would be done.

I asked if he had done this himself. He replied, "Repeatedly, but nothing happened." Maybe he was too timid or had been sold weak or fake arsenic. He said that as a good son I should do it. Obviously, we certainly disagreed on this and he shouted at me that I was not a good son if I didn't do it. But I held my ground. At the end of my visit, I quietly took the arsenic with me when we left for the airport. After he dropped me off at O'Hare I dumped the poison in a garbage bin. He soon discovered it was gone, and I got a call from him raising hell about it.

Next fall coming back from Moscow having coached the USA Team at the 1975 World Weightlifting Championships, I stayed with him for a few days and we went through the whole scenario again.

The fall before, in 1974, when he had first revealed the arsenic plan, he was taking heavy tranquilizers (Librium) that made him pass out for about 15-20 minutes sometimes. He said he needed them to calm him down and to get a little sleep, which he couldn't do. He took a lot of them as he said he was still not drinking. In 1975, he must have been taking even more of them as they were stashed all over the place—in car seats, in the condo, and the office. His office manager, Audrey Johnson, thought he would kill himself driving under the influence of those pills.

He was always agitated. He said he had a very understanding physician, Jimmy Stack, whom I knew very well from the fifties and sixties. I asked Dr. Stack why he did this. He said, "Your dad is a very strong-willed person, and he will come out of this. But it's either the tranquilizers or drinking."

Back when we were on the way back from O'Hare into town in 1975 the first thing he wanted to do was stop at a real sleazy Turkish bathhouse on Division Street, that has since been torn down. It was one of the worst places I've been in, and I've been all over South America in some terrible slums and in Calcutta, India, where I saw people being picked up on the streets after they died in their own filth. At the bathhouse I met King Solomon, who was downright slime.

For $50,000 in cash from my dad, King Solomon gave him very strong arsenic. My dad asked, "Are you sure this is strong enough?" King Solomon said, "Stronger than all the other batches I gave you, but you chickened out. Now do it!" My dad said, "This is my son who will do it."

King Solomon said, "Good, because you owe me more money than this."

Well, it was the same scene as the previous year: showing me what to do, repeatedly saying he can't do this. He was insistent that it had to be done. He was a self-made man, and he couldn't give her half the money nor could he live with her. I argued with him and we shouted at each other. "You're not being a good son!" He was miserable with his situation and this time he told me I would get $100,000 up front for doing it. I refused and again snagged the arsenic and dumped it at O'Hare. This whole thing was shocking to me—to think he wanted me to kill her for him.

Events became even more bizarre in the fall of 1975. I kept getting telephone calls from my dad's office manager Audrey Johnson saying that King Solomon's nephew came up to the office looking for my dad claiming he owed him thousands of dollars. He terrorized the office with his irrational ranting and bloody appearance. Apparently someone had beat him up badly, even one of his eyes was half out. Audrey Johnson threatened to quit over these events and others. Dad hired, I seem to remember, Dan Murphy, one of his old pals who'd been his bodyguard previously, to protect him and the office from King Solomon's thugs. Dan was a former Chicago Police detective and a member of Chicago's North Side Mafia. Bernie Lindquist, one of my dad's best friends, confirmed this. Interestingly, King Solomon's nephew died within a day or two of my father.

My dad had put Audrey Johnson in a difficult position. He told people that if anybody needed to know what was going on in the office or where to find him they should ask Audrey because she knew everything. Audrey thought she was followed for two years, probably by Dan Murphy. She didn't go out at night. When she went to work an old truck was always parked outside her house. It was there at night, too. She also thought she was followed when she was on the train or bus. She felt that my dad had her tailed so the wrong people wouldn't find out about him.

Also in the fall of 1975, Dad wanted me to drive to Virginia and attend an insurance conference for him. I did and when I came back he was furious when I told him the direction the insurance business was going. I mention this because he wasn't drinking so this must have been something he really disagreed with.

Around December of 1975 I asked Dad how his liver was, and he said it was great. Since he had now stopped drinking for over four years his liver tests were coming out excellent.

Late in 1975 and early 1976, Dad needed money so he decided to try to get back some expensive jewelry he had given to a woman he had once dated named Frankie Howard. Believe it or not, he also wanted jewelry that other men had given her. So my dad, Frankie, and I went to lunch at the Drake Hotel one day, and he just came out and told her he wanted the jewelry. He said, "I'm a nice guy but my son isn't, and he'll come after you when I am dead and kill you." He wanted that jewelry whether he was alive or not. I guess she thought I wasn't fearsome enough to carry out this threat because she never gave any of the jewelry back. She was attractive, tall, brownish blonde hair, but was in it for what she could get out of it—very manipulative and false. At one time my dad was completely infatuated with her. He was even seeing her while married to Marilyn. But that all stopped when Marilyn died in the car accident.

Later on, in January 1976, he said he wanted to branch out in insurance and he came to Santa Fe and Albuquerque to see if he wanted to buy an insurance agency owned by Buster Quest, a former Olympic javelin thrower. I mention this because we spent about five days together and he drank nothing so I assume he was thinking rationally. He did take plenty of Librium, although not as much as I had seen him take before.

He had the idea that he'd start fresh, buy an insurance agency near me and have me run it. Then he'd eventually move out to New Mexico. Although I had worked for him three summers when I was in college, I had told him I never wanted to go into business with him. Upon this request of his, though, I decided to look into it with him because I was concerned about his mental anguish, and I hoped this would distract him from killing his wife Matt. But he thought about it and in February he called me up and said he just couldn't go through with purchasing Quest's agency and making such a major move. I could sense that he was taking more of the Librium than ever.

Then in April of 1976 Matt called and wanted to know what a big, unidentifiable pill was doing in a certain cupboard. I said "I don't know, why?" She said she knew about my dad's tranquilizers because they were stashed all over the house, but this was something new and looked nothing like those pills. She must have suspected he was trying to harm or kill her. She came right out and asked, "Is he trying to do something to me?" I have had some foul tasting tea and coffee in the last couple of years." I told her I didn't know anything.

I found out many years later that in April 1976 my dad retained a new lawyer and revised his will. More on that later!

In June of 1976, two months after Matt asked me about the pill she couldn't identify, Lynn and I were driving to the Olympic weightlifting trials. I stopped around two in the afternoon and called dad from a gas station in. I called him regularly as he was so distraught and I was fearful of his life. He sounded miserable, as usual, and I asked him if he was taking the Librium, and he said he was. I also asked him if he was still off the booze and he confessed that he was drinking a little. I asked what a little was and he said about two glasses of Hiram-Deluxe and water nightly. And he'd started doing it in late May. I mention this because I had called him many nights, including late May, and he was not drunk. I could always tell when he had been drinking heavily. He said he was having trouble with King Solomon because he owed him so much money for arsenic. I asked if he was still buying and trying the arsenic, and he said he wasn't and that it was useless." But then he said he was trying something that was undetectable.

I called him later that night when we got to my brother-in-law's house in Tulsa. When I asked him how he was doing, for the first time in ages he said he was "doing fine and just trying to get a little sleep, son." Two hours later, Matt called and said he was dead

We left for Chicago that morning and met with various people, including Terry (Terrell) Isselhard, the new attorney he'd retained a couple of months before. At the Wake, King Solomon, the slime ball, came up to me and told me that my dad owed him $50,000. He wanted that money, and he said if I didn't give it to him, he would harm my wife and two children. Before and after the funeral, Isselhard assured me I shouldn't worry about the will as I would get a lot of money. The will would not be ready for a couple of weeks, however, so I had no idea what it contained. Isselhard was the one who revised the will. However, his statement that I would get a lot of money turned out to be misleading.

We left Chicago for the Olympic trials in Philadelphia, and then after the tryouts and the training camp we left for Montreal, Canada for the Olympic Games. I called Terry Isselhard during the games, and he said things still were not settled, but that I shouldn't worry. Later, I met Rosemary Martin, who would be carrying out the will's instructions regarding the disbursement of money.

As it turned out, dad left me no money in the will. Instead, I would have access to funds for education and welfare if I requested it. Then, I applied to the University of New Mexico Medical School to study to become an orthopedic surgeon. My background would serve me well as a doctor. After I was admitted, I asked Rosemary Martin for money for medical school as the will stated that education was a valid reason for assistance. She said "The Committee" would have to decide. This turned out to be one of many requests that was denied because "The Committee" said no. So that was the end of that.

Many years later, one of the requests that was funded was financial assistance for my son Kyle when he went to Stanford. Stanford awarded Kyle a partial scholarship for half his expenses and between the trust and myself, the balance was covered.

After the Olympic Games in 1976 I went to Los Angeles to be with Dad's mother, my grandmother, for several weeks. She told me then and again in 1982 that Matt was going to get all the money, and if she weren't so tired she would go to Chicago and fight for my rights. It seems that Dad had laid out certain terms in his will leaving some money ($325,000) in trust and some cash to my grandmother. The rest was left in trust to Matt. When my grandmother died, she left me the cash. In the end I got about $60,000 after fees were subtracted. Of that, I gave $15,000 to my mother and $15,000 to my stepfather.

When I got back from visiting my grandmother a persistent King Solomon kept calling and asking for the $50,000 or he would "get my family." At that point I wasn't that concerned about it.

Later in 1976, I learned the stated cause of my father's death. According to Terry Isselhard, Matt had attributed his demise to cirrhosis of the liver. I was suspicious of this right away because my father had laid off alcohol for several years and was only drinking lightly at the time of his death. Moreover, when someone dies of cirrhosis of the liver I understand that the last five to ten days are very painful, and the person is usually admitted to the hospital because he can no longer care for himself. It seemed to me that my dad's health was fine the morning of his death. He had been at the office and he and Audrey Johnson had an argument. She said she didn't notice anything unusual about his appearance or attitude at the time. Arguments were the norm when dealing with him so an argument was not unusual.

In the late 1980s I went to the Cook County Courthouse to examine official reports on my father's death. It seems that a police officer at the scene had asked Matt what was the cause of death? She had answered that it was cirrhosis of the liver. She had been drunk at the time. I also learned, to my astonishment, that no autopsy was performed even though the law requires an autopsy when a death occurs outside a hospital. According to the reports that were on file, a blood test was taken. Some, but not a high level of alcohol was found. No drugs were in the bloodstream even though Dad said he had taken five or six Librium the afternoon of his death.

After I had discovered the statements concerning my dad's death, I called Matt and boldly asked her, "Why did you kill him?" To my surprise she replied, "He had it coming." I then told her what I knew about the pill she had once asked me about. I could tell she was really drunk so I got no response.

Jumping ahead, in the early 1990s I contacted people I was sure knew about Dad's bizarre attempts on Matt's life. One of his friends living in Chicago told me that the pill Matt had found back in April 1976, two months before my dad died, was "the magic pill" containing a poison that couldn't be detected.

Why did I think a number of people would know about my dad's reprehensible actions? Because he was very blunt and never hesitated to tell me and his close friends all the despicable things he had done. Part of the reason was his feeling that his friends were loyal. He valued loyalty very much. His arrogance made him feel that he was untouchable and that his friends would never betray him no matter what he did.

Soon after I had contacted these people, I had a personal visit in Santa Fe from a man claiming to be King Solomon's son. He was determined to get the $50,000 owed to his father from the arsenic days. Through some contacts and elaborate maneuvering, I was able to have him apprehended in Bernalillo, New Mexico. When the police checked his record, it turned out he was wanted in Chicago for drug trafficking. (See details in "King Solomon" later in this book.)

Time goes on. I had learned that there had been no test for oxygen level in the blood even though Matt had asked if asphyxiation could be detected. Why wasn't there an autopsy to determine whether he died of cirrhosis of the liver, a very serious and debilitating condition? Why wasn't the oxygen content in his blood ascertained when his wife asked such a revealing question? Why wasn't someone—his doctor, close friends, office personnel—suspicious of the circumstances?

Alternative Explanations, My Tentative Conclusions, Further Thoughts

My dad might have been suffocated to death. He became very placid if he had a drink (and he said he was taking Librium) and could have been suffocated by someone. Maybe he went to bed before his wife, which was not unusual, and she smothered him while he was vulnerable from sleep and the effects of alcohol.

My dad possibly died from arsenic poisoning. Arsenic was in the house. He had said he was trying to kill Matt, but maybe she found it and used it on him. There is no evidence, however, that his health deteriorated as it would have if the arsenic had been added to his food or drink over a period of days or weeks. If he had been given a massive dose the evening I talked to him, his peaceful attitude was not consistent with such poisoning.

My dad committed suicide by arsenic or other means. Again, although the arsenic would have caused very painful symptoms that isn't consistent with his mental and physical state a couple of hours before he died. Maybe he had taken something else that calmed him, then used arsenic or something else later to kill himself. Unlikely. But someone knew the answer because I remember being told by a number of people to keep quiet and that I would get nothing if the cause of death was not natural since insurance wouldn't be honored under that condition.

My dad died of other means. I was told by one of his friends in 1989 that Dad told him he had located a pill that was undetectable and that he was doing to kill Matt with it, the so-called "Magic Pill." Matt had called in April 1976 wanting information on the pill she had found. So, Matt could have given him that pill, or he could have taken it himself.

Matt did in fact kill my father, but it was an accident. They could have had a fight. She might have put a pillow over his head to keep him quiet. She didn't mean to kill him. But, if he was coherent enough to argue with her, how could she suffocate a conscious, strong man without a battle. Did he pass out for some reason (drugs, alcohol), and then she saw her chance?

Why would my Dad leave virtually everything to the person he was trying to kill? He did not even allow me, my wife, and my two kids to inherit the trust he left my grandmother while Matt was alive. Some of Dad's friends told me he felt I could take care of myself, but that Matt couldn't take care of herself.

Cirrhosis of the liver is usually a process where, when the liver begins to fail, the person becomes very ill and has be hospitalized. Usually the person dies in a matter of days. My dad died suddenly. Did Matt lie to the police? Did my dad lie to her and tell her he had this condition?

I was distraught in August 1989 when I learned of the inquest, no autopsy, and other things Matt had said. As I mentioned earlier, I had called her and actually asked her if she had killed my father. Later I wrote her a letter stating that no matter what had gone on in the past, what was done was done, and the whole situation was sick and that I had saved her life because I refused to put arsenic in her tea leaves. She again told me "He had it coming" and she had before and to never call her, that my father (as she had told me many times before) had hated me, thought nothing of me, and that she would have me arrested if I called again. Matt died in the spring of 1995 and all the money was left to Northwestern and Yale universities.

In late 1996, Rosemary Martin called and said there was $25,000 left over from Dad's estate. She kept $5,000 and sent the remainder to my sons, Kyle and Shane.

King Solomon and the Aftermath

To recap, in the foyer at Dad's funeral, as I said earlier, King Solomon approached me and demanded $50,000 which he said my dad owed him. I said I knew nothing about that and was never given any money by my dad. Seems he had been going to my dad's office when he wasn't there, which terrorized the office. He kept calling me weekly for the money.

My dad had employed Dan Murphy, former part of the Northside Irish mafia as I mentioned earlier. So what I did was hire the same Dan Murphy to protect my family in Santa Fe. I did this for two years and it cost me a lot of money. It was after those two years that King Solomon died. I thought I was through with him but that was not the case. Some years later after Sandra and I were married and had our gym, I got a phone call. Sandra was at the gym and this was about five in the afternoon. The man on the phone asked if I remembered him. I didn't and he asked if he could come over. I told him to come ahead.

Turns out he was king Solomon's son and he too wanted the $50,000 that his dad must have told him about. I said, "I know nothing about this." But he insisted on the money or he was going to kill me unless he got it. I suddenly thought of a plan. I figured he probably had drugs in his car so I told him the money was on the south side of town. My plan was to speed south through Santa Fe in the hopes that the police would stop me for speeding and then I would tell the policeman what was going on and they would arrest him for drug possession. I told him to follow me. Well, I went at a high rate of speed through Santa Fe but no police in sight. I continued speeding and headed for Albuquerque. I thought for sure the State Police would catch me along with King Solomon's son. Finally, they did when we were about fifty miles out of town.

The State Police officer searched both our cars and found weed and heroin in King Solomon's son's car. He arrested him, made a phone call and confirmed that this man was wanted in Chicago for possession and distribution of drugs. The officer cuffed him and he was soon sent back to Chicago. I kept in touch with Chicago's drug department, phoning every six months. He was in jail for five years and I was told he died there. That was the end of an era I was glad to be rid of.

My Stepfather

Lenard Kenith McRae, "Mac," my stepfather, was what you call the strong and silent type. He had a large influence on my life because of who he was. He was raised in Fargo, North Dakota. His father was Scottish and his mother Welch. His father was a bank accountant and did well financially until he died early of pancreatic cancer. Mac was the second of two boys. His brother, Courney, was two years his elder and was a big drinker and a real trouble maker. Pop, my name for him, had to get him out of fights constantly. By the time Courney was in high school he was drinking heavily. His mother, Ida, always favored him.

Pop never drank and was very devotional, going to church three times a week. He was not into religion but went to church to please his mother. But it didn't seem to get his mother to like him better and he didn't understand this.

Both boys were good athletes and musicians. Pop played trombone in the high school band. He also played football as a receiving end and linebacker. When he wasn't playing football or baseball he was practicing the trombone a couple of hours a day. He was so good that he received a music scholarship to the University of North Dakota. He was also offered a football scholarship, but he chose music and played trombone in various bands. Following his father's early death, he quit school to earn as much money as he could to support his mother and brother.

When Pop was in high school he also did a lot of farming and cattle herding. He loved the round ups but he once got bitten by a rattle snake while he was sleeping and this was enough to turn him away from a future in cattle herding. Instead, he concentrated on getting his degree in accounting and was a bank examiner for years until he was drafted in the Army Air Corps.

During WWII he went to flight school to become a paratrooper and completed his training in England. Jumping out of planes was something he really enjoyed. He was in the invasion of Normandy on June 6, 1944. A time came when the Nazis had so much success shooting the paratroopers down that his group switched to a glider. That was no picnic, as the Nazis put stakes in the open ground and flooded the fields. But his glider landed successfully.

Meanwhile, six days after the invasion Mac and his buddy were standing on a log in St. Moritz, France when they heard mortar fire. Pop ran one way and his partner went the other. Suddenly a piece of shrapnel hit Pop, taking off half his right knee. He was quickly put onto an airplane and flown to England. He had several operations and spent nine months in a British hospital recuperating before being sent home. When they dismissed him they told him that he would have to work that knee every day if he wanted to keep his leg. He was used to exercise since he had been active in sports early on, but now the sport was to save his leg, which he did.

But years later, when he was 85 the knee started to hurt and swell. As it turned out, he had an infection which had to be cut out. Apparently he had been harboring that infection since1944, an amazing length of time. That it was found at all was a God send. He lived to be 92 when he died of prostate cancer, but the lower leg was still working.

He had graduated with an accounting degree to become a CPA and when the depression was over he married my mom whom he had previously met in Chicago. They went to Los Angeles and then right to the San Fernando Valley where, even after they divorced, she lived for the rest of her life. They had one daughter named Kathleen, after the boat they had spent their honeymoon on.

What I learned from him was to plan carefully and pay attention to details once a path is chosen. I learned the importance of mastering every detail. You know some people usually make great plans but don't pay attention to details. And then there are people who can't see the overall picture.

One thing worth mentioning about Pop that surprised all of us was how he could create things—for example, hat racks. No one would have imagined that he would be interested in that, let alone know how to do it!

After he and my mom divorced he lived in the Saugus Desert in an old, smoky trailer for over twenty years, but later moved to Las Vegas and bought a new condo. He fixed it up and had a good time doing it. And he was proud of what he had done. Previously, he rarely had anybody over, but after fixing up the place he had people over three to four times a week. He kept it pristine and didn't allow smoking.

When I look through his life I can see he was the kind of person who could say and feel that there were stages to his life—this is one part, and then now here is another part. He recognized and enjoyed dramatically different stages and versions of his life.

He really loved his daughter Kathleen and the real reason he moved to Las Vegas was to protect her. It seems somebody was after her and he felt she needed his protection. She was very close to him as well and took great care of him when his health failed.

The last weekend he was alive I flew to Las Vegas to see him. He really enjoyed it, but kept asking Kathleen why I came. She kept saying, "Because he loves you." It was like he couldn't accept this. But then most of his life he couldn't understand why so many people loved him. I believe he finally did understand and was at real peace with this.

My Sister Kathleen McCrae

Kathleen has been a dental hygienist and then a medical office manager. She has two great children who now have families of their own. They now live in Colorado and for the first time we all live fairly close to each other. She is very talented, especially in dance. Her dancing ability and willingness to teach me has been a big part of my closeness to my wife, Sandra. Through dancing we have really gotten to know each while having fun. Dancing is a great bond between us and brings us closer together.

My Son Shane

Shane was born in 1968. He was very good in football as an end. He has great hands and always enjoyed art. In fact, he went to the University of New Mexico on an art scholarship. He likes music and has cut a couple of good albums. He was always interested in the sport of lifting and continued to lift in college and upon graduating from college. He enjoyed teaching the Olympic lifts and helping people get in shape. After college he was with us in the gym for over twenty years and then, unfortunately, we had a parting of the ways and he started his own Olympic-style gym in Santa Fe.

This book was hard to write because I have to remember back sixty-five plus years and for me it is hard to recall certain times and details. A challenge that is rewarding but stressful. To recall exactly I rely on my wife Sandra and a lot from my second son Kyle. It would have been better if I could have asked my son Shane but maybe some day things will work out. Being with him in the gym was good and we had planned to eventually turn the gym over to him. But he seems to have his own independent life now and as a result, we ended up in the same town running our own individual gyms.

My Son Kyle

Kyle was born in 1970. When Kyle was in the fifth grade I taught him and six other students to play chess at Carlos Gilbert School. Kyle practiced two to three hours every day—sometimes in the bathtub! He became very skilled at it. Although he had no formal coaching, he won the state championship against a young man, Andy Fisher, who had a full time coach for years. He raised money and traveled all over the country competing in chess tournaments against the best. I say he saw more of the country than I did as the USA Olympic Weightlifting Coach. In his senior year he won the national high school chess championship and he and his teammates placed second in the nation in chess championships. They were the Santa Fe High School team. He also played soccer and was picked for an All State Team. Some people stop when they reach their best. He did drop chess but won a scholarship to play varsity soccer at Stanford as a sweeper. The summer before he went to Stanford I raced him every day. I started that summer beating him by two-three yards in the forty yard dash. At the end of the summer he was beating me by the same distance.

His major at Stanford was German and Political Science. He also studied in France and got his Masters in Business Administration before working at a bank in Berlin for two years. He then returned to Santa Fe and worked for us for a few months and then moved to San Jose to work for Ernst and Young in International Tax specializing in expatriate tax returns. He continues to play soccer—once a week for a men's team and once a week on a coed team.

When Kyle was in France we visited him in Toulouse. He took us around and we very much enjoyed this charming city with its fine bread and cheeses. We didn't, however, enjoy the round intersections, which to us were slow and jammed up with bumper to bumper cars.

My Wife Sandra

To me, Sandra had a special childhood, growing up in Sault Sainte Marie in the Upper Peninsula of Michigan. Her father was a violinist and taught music and had a music store. She had wonderful neighbors, swam in the Great Lakes, and ice skated. In her senior year of high school, Sandra spent a year in Austria as an exchange student. She got along well with the other students. But the adults had a superiority attitude and they still discussed WWII in a very arrogant way. I felt much the same about the older Japanese. It was like they could do it all over again. I could be wrong.

Sandra's father had a band, orchestras and choirs—both in Michigan and then later in Long Beach, California. Sandra concentrated on the piano and is excellent. At one time, after not playing the piano for some thirty years, she took it up again and practiced enough to put on a performance of Beethoven's Piano Sonata No. 23 in F minor, Op. 57 (the *Appassionata*) which was appreciated by an audience of over two hundred. Sandra has taught me a lot about classical music and I have really enjoyed it.

Sandra's son from a previous marriage, Chris, lifts weights and was a youth minister and at the time this book was published is a hospice chaplain in Bryan, Texas. While he was a youth minister, he played all kinds of sports with his young adults. Her daughter, Shara is a great hiker and skis extremely well. It is remarkable to see Sandra and Shara enjoy hiking and skiing together. A few years ago they went to New Zealand and hiked three of the Great Walks together and had a wonderful time. Shara is an art therapist at Gunnison College in Colorado. Sandra has a close relationship with Shara and they are always sharing ideas and thoughts. It is heart warming to be around them both. Once Sandra built a yurt with

Shara and her boyfriend on Sandra's land just over the border in Pagosa Springs, Colorado. There is a lake there called William Lake where Shara kayaks and hikes. It is just as pristine as Abiquiu Lake in New Mexico. Both Chris and Shara are fine people in spirit and in their careers.

Sandra is a born teacher and an excellent dancer. She taught elementary school and junior and senior high school math. She currently teaches Zumba at the gym one day a week and works miracles teaching our individual programs and has done so for the last several decades. She also does individual work with the elderly both at the gym and sometimes in their homes.

One of our big entertainments is ballroom dancing and we go about two or three Saturdays a month at our famous Santa Fe hotel, La Fonda. People enjoy watching Sandra dance. She can really move. As I mentioned earlier, dancing has really drawn us together. Powerful! Living in Santa Fe we have gotten into Latin dancing but our favorite has always been rhythm and blues.

Sandra is also good at snow skiing and water ballet. Watching her perform is like poetry in motion. About five years ago she bought a kayak and when ski season is over she takes the kayak up to Lake Abiquiu, about an hour and fifteen minutes away from Santa Fe and kayaks for four or five hours. And she is an expert in hiking and climbing.

We built our log home in the foothills of Santa Fe. It is open concept with lots of windows and skylights. Rooms are large and few. The kids are gone so we built it with this in mind. Our living area is big with wooden floors just great for dancing. And we also go dancing at a few places in town other than La Fonda—lots of rhythm and blues and salsa. We have built a small pond below our log home and ten yards to right of that is a regulation, all cement badminton court. We tried to grow a garden but at eight thousand feet elevation, there are too many animals which made it impossible, so that's the reason for the badminton court. We even have it lit so we can play at night. Lots of fun. It was a childhood game for both our families when we were growing up. We found that badminton is a game most people can learn easily and well. It takes too much coordination to play tennis, so badminton it is! Once in a while, Sandra manages to beat me.

Our driveway is curved, not very wide and about fifty yards long.

Many times I have accidentally backed up off the driveway into the arroyo. My car towing man (yes, I have a car towing man!) Nelson Flores used to kid me about the many times I went off the driveway backing up.

I had a VW bus from 1998 (when "Star Wars" came out) to 2001 (when the Trade Centers came down). It could only go in reverse and first gear and it would be too costly to fix it so I decided to donate it. A non-profit organization in Santa Fe called Esperanza, which means hope, had been advertising on the radio asking people to donate vehicles, even if they didn't work. I contacted them solidly for six months but I couldn't get them to come take a look at it, so I gave it to one of the workers at the gym. Good riddance.

We read a lot, especially historical novels. It's fun and informative to read about a person in the times and places where they were. Sandra reads even more than I do, about as much as my trainer and Olympic Champion, Frank Spellman did. Which is saying a lot! She comes weekly with armful of books from the gym book table—about three books at a time.

We still train. I recently did two power cleans from the floor with 292 pounds. I have Parkinson's Disease which adversely affects my balance so I don't split or squat. At the time this book was published I was 78 and weighed 197. Besides weight training I walk up and down hills outside our house four days a week. I do power cleans twice a week, along with stair climbing for twenty minutes, leg kicks for the stomach, hamstring stretches and bar squats for twenty minutes. For the rest of my workout I concentrate on balance exercises for my Parkinson's. I also hike once or twice a week with Sandra. She has hiked up and down the Sangre de Cristos from five in the morning to six in the evening and hiked twenty-six miles across the Sandia Mountains outside of Albuquerque. At the age of 76 she is in top shape. She has great form in Snatch and Clean and Jerk.

Traveling with Sandra

Sandra and I like to travel. After visiting my son Kyle in France as I mentioned earlier, we drove to Pisa and on to Florence. We made Florence our headquarters in Italy and went all over, including Rome and Milan and Venice. In Venice we were standing in a museum line when we heard OJ Simpson had been found not guilty of murdering Nicole and Ron Goldman. We thought it was a joke and so did many of the Italians. When we returned to Santa Fe, I called up my good friend Al Vermeil, who worked for the Chicago Bulls when OJ was playing. I asked Al what he thought of Simpson and he said he didn't believe Simpson could have killed them.

We once made a trip to Costa Rica during the time when the Sandinistas were in control of Nicaragua. Much earlier I had taken a team to two Central American countries, one being Nicaragua and I had kept up a correspondence with two of their lifters. On the way to Costa Rica I was happy to know we were going to have a layover of four or five hours. I asked the military who met and surrounded our plane if they knew of John Santos and Henry Archula. They said they did and agreed to tell them I was at the airport for a short time and would like to see them. About an hour before we left, the two lifters drove up in a military bus. We talked for about forty-five minutes and they told me how much progress they had made in their lifting but the government wouldn't let them travel outside the country because it felt they would try and escape. They said they were constantly watched but were fed well and they trained two or three hours a day. Their parents and brothers and sisters, however, were not fed well and lived in dirty conditions. Sounded like what the Cuban lifters said once when I talked to them on phone, one living in Florida and the other in Las Vegas, Nevada.

It was good to see and talk with them. Later I was surprised when they started writing to me. They had to be careful and I also as the letters were read by Nicaraguan government. I hadn't heard from them after about three years and I finally received a letter saying their parents were tortured to death because they had stopped working at hard labor. They must have been close to eighty years old.

From Nicaragua, we flew to Costa Rica. It was very beautiful and the people were charming. The atmosphere was entirely different from Nicaragua. After about a week of further observation and having talked to people of all occupational jobs we got the idea that the Sandinistas did not come into Costa Rica because about ninety percent of the Costa Ricans had their own homes and they were content. So there wasn't much they could be offered. And freedom was everywhere. Heck, the

Costa Ricans didn't even have a military. It reminded me of Switzerland. Nobody bothered the Swiss or the Costa Ricans. As an aside, Costa Rica has the greatest variety of birds in the world and people come from all over to see them.

While we were there we befriended a young man who was returning to Costa Rica to go to work at his family's businesses. He had graduated from a university in New Jersey in engineering. His family was throwing a celebration party for him and he and family invited Sandra and me to come. All types of food were served. A big favorite was roasted pig. There were lots of relatives, and all were friendly to each other and to Sandra and me. The party went on for two days with eating, drinking, dancing and soccer with American football and volleyball as well. After about two days, the celebration subsided. Everyone was exhausted.

We then walked for two days throughout the capital, San Jose. The east coast waters were calm and easy to snorkel and enjoy all the fish and coral. The west coast, on the other hand, had great waves and was ideal for surfing.

On the west coast we rented a room from a retired black missionary couple. The price was right and the food good and any time we went into the water to snorkel or walk into the rain forest they always made sure we had bananas to take with us and they worried about us. I corresponded with them for about half a year. Their room was across the street from two bars that constantly played music till dawn. Sandra called it the battle of the bands!

On another trip to the Caribbean we went to Belize. We snorkeled and saw many nurse sharks and huge turtles. We rented a tent on an island in Belize. There was a young couple there who were hired to keep the tent grounds safe. After about the third night we left a dance to turn in for the night. After I had gone to sleep I woke up to a tearing sound. Two young men with a knife were trying to get into the tent to steal from us but Sandra and I changed their minds. I fought them until they finally got tired and left. Our young couple in charge hired a policeman for the next two nights. No Problem! So we felt safe enough.

We then flew out to Houston and stayed a couple of days and nights in that city. Years before, I had gone to Houston to see some potential Olympic weightlifters. Their coach was Otto Ziegler. At this point in time

Otto was ninety-one but he loved life and was full of it. When I had been traveling the country I met many older coaches who were happy that I was there because up until then nobody had come to them and encouraged them and helped their programs. (More on this later.)

Another time we went to Aruba. We had a lifter at our gym named Ed Vissa. His family lived there and we met them. They had multiple businesses and showed us all of them and their family. They also told us that the island was a big narcotics place for drugs. There is also a small island off Aruba called Bonaire with the same drug scene, we were told. Apparently the drugs came from Colombia.

On another trip to the Caribbean we went to St. Johns Island but the people were not too friendly and the newspaper there reported a killing a day. We also went to Cancun, Mexico. Lots of fun people, lots of beach volleyball and great food. And good bands to dance to.

Once on my way back from India to Japan, I made a stop in Hawaii because World and Olympic Champions Tommy Kono and Peter George lived there. Growing up around Frank Spellman I had heard a lot about them. Their experiences in the World and Olympic Championships were memorable to me.

And then there was one very special trip—Sault Sainte Marie in the Upper Peninsula of Michigan where Sandra grew up. I could go on and on, but I think you get the idea that we like to travel. Enough said.

2

Early Influences

When I was in elementary school through high school I was very good in science, math, and English composition. In athletics I was all city (Los Angeles) in football as a quarterback. My other athletic interest was surfing because I had good balance. And I had continued to progress in Olympic-style lifting under the coaching of Frank Spellman, 1948 Middleweight Olympic Champion. In college I continued in lifting, played quarterback, threw javelin, and discus.

Football and High School Coach Sweed O'Halloran

Growing up in the Los Angeles area we sometimes played teams in the Watts area. One time playing football I threw a pass and was immediately hit. Then one of the opposing player walked over my back. The referee called a penalty for unnecessary roughness. The player told the ref, "Man, he's got shoulder pads on." Not meaning anything about it, but I have to say that was the attitude in that area at the time so we just made the best of it.

Growing up, we read a lot of strength and health magazines. Frequently there were articles on the Russians eating two grams of protein for every pound of body weight. I weighed at that time 190 pounds. So times two and you can see I was eating 380 grams of protein a day. I felt terrible. I was bloated and tired all the time. Finally I said to myself that I just don't care what the Russians are doing, I won't do it. Later on when I was coaching and went to Russia, they told me that they had told the magazines many things that weren't true.

When I was playing football in high school as a quarterback our coach was a small, red-haired young man named Sweed O'Halloran. He was very talented and, in addition to football tactics, he taught me to be flexible in my thinking. And he used humor—good clean humor. To me playing quarterback was a serious matter and keeping a sense of humor under his influence was a real help. I think he picked up his focus on humor by watching TV shows and reading books.

Years after high school I asked him, "Sweed, how did you come to believe that humor was so good in coaching?" He said that humor takes the edge off and thus makes one play better. I remember two games where this really came home to me. In one game I threw five interceptions. We were first in our league until that game. For the next game Sweed went over a lot of his own personal experiences with humor with me. I ended up throwing a game winning touchdown. Before the game I had felt great, relaxed and focused because of what he said.

Bert Goodrich Gym, Muscle Beach and Frank Spellman

I was happy playing football, baseball and tennis. My stepdad had said if he wanted to save his lower leg (remember his knee was badly injured in WWII) he would have to exercise it for the rest of life. And that is how we started weight training. We commuted three days a week to Hollywood where the famous Bert Goodrich, the first Mr. America, had a gym on Hollywood Boulevard. We trained there for three years.

Here's the weight training scene at the time as seen through the eyes of a twelve to seventeen year old: There was an eclectic bunch of members at the gym, many of them famous. Two were nationally known pro wrestlers named Baron Michele Leone and Lord James Blears. They were on TV all the time. Others included Mario Lanza the opera star, Steve Reeves who played a Tarzan-like character is a movie, Marilyn Monroe, Jayne Mansfield, Mal Whitfield the 400 and 800 meter Olympic champion, Beverly Clark, Pudge and Les Stockston, Perry Obrian, Vic and Armon Tanny, and Jack LaLane.

Some of these people trained at Muscle Beach in Santa Monica. There were top Olympic weightlifters like Frank Spellman, Isaac Berger, Dave Sheppard, and Bob Hoffman who owned York Barbell in York, Pennsylvania who came with some of his Olympic hopefuls. There they had strange weight games, like running forty yards in the sand carrying 35 to 50 pound barbells. Jimmy Lee, the Olympic sprint champion, would race 370 pound Paul Anderson who won the heavyweight Olympic Championship in Melbourne, Australia. Paul would lose by just a step to Jimmy Lee in the 40 yard dash. The whole scene was super fun. But about two or three years later, it developed into a terrible atmosphere with drugs and alcohol and the city closed it down.

It was at Bert's gym that I met Frank Spellman, 1948 Olympic Weightlifting Champion, middle weight class 165 pounds. He still weighed the same at the time at 94 years old. Frank took a liking to me and my stepdad. Our homes were close to each other and since the gym was some distance away from where we lived, Frank suggested we train in his garage which he had converted into a gym even though the ceiling was low. We had to be careful when doing the jerk not to hit it! That was fun, and Frank attracted great athletes like Dave Davis, Dallas Long, Parry O'Brien and Jay Silvestor—all of whom went to the Olympics. Then there was Paul Anderson, Pete George, and Dave Sheppard. Others included Bob Hoffman, Dave Maggard, John Terpak, Mabel and Perry Rader, Bob Hise, and Tommy Kono. Also Harold Sakata, John Davis, and Bob Mathias. Top weightlifting officials also came.

Frank Spellman was raised in an orphanage in Pennsylvania. He took advantage of everything they offered, including art and learning how to play many musical instruments. He didn't complain about any injuries he had from his intense lifting—instead he did something about them, and he would heal up. He was a wonderful human being with a joyful, fun, caring character– always upbeat, praising people. He was always interested in people—how they are doing in any part of their lives, including their families. He always had something kind to say about them after a conversation. He would often say about a person, "He was trying always to do good." And he meant it. If a person didn't enter a competition, Frank would say "He's just resting." Everywhere I went in weightlifting, the name Frank Spellman opened doors.

Back in 1948, Khadr El-Touni of Egypt was the favorite to win in his weightlifting class at the Olympics. But Frank Spellman had a perfect day, didn't miss a lift. Frank took first and his teammate, Pete George, took second; El-Touni was third.

Frank died at the age of 94. He was always enthusiastic. He said as you get older you need to keep up your interest in things. For example, he painted very well, played piano, kettle drums, trumpet, xylophone and harpsichord. He was a voracious reader and was very inquisitive.

Bob Hoffman, Bob Hise and the York Barbell Team

Many of us when we were growing up lifted in garages and pur-chased good Olympic sets. One of the best was from Bob Hoffman in York, Pennsylvania. Bob Hoffman was called The Father of Olympic weight lifting in the US. He started in the 1930s. Then in the 1970s Bob Hise started selling his Olympic sets which were also very good. Like Hoffman, Hise sponsored lifters and after a decade beat what Bob Hoffman called the York Barbell team. That was the first time ever that the York Barbell team had been beaten. My coach Frank Spellman worked for Bob Hoffman for seven year before moving to the Los Angeles area. Frank told me a lot about Bob Hoffman and the York Barbell business and teams. Everyone had a job there. Frank had been a screw mechanic. The lifters trained at various times. Bob would work out on a schedule and Bob would come in and coach him at least two times a week. Bob coached lifters at various times, depending on their work hours.

Bob Hise tried this on a few of his lifters depending on how well they could do. The company was called Maverick. Bob did this until his death from pancreatic cancer. Bob's son and fellow employee Herb Glassbrenner also did this for a few years but they just didn't have the skill to continue what Bob Hise Sr. had started. It takes a tremendous amount of skill and energy to run such a business.

One of the things Hoffman did was put out a monthly magazine called *Strength and Health*. It was very successful because of its articles and Bob knew how to get it distributed across the country. The magazine also was good for getting the word out about his line of products, which included all sorts of Olympic sets from dumb bells to ordinary barbells.

You knew you had arrived in weightlifting when you got your picture on the cover of that magazine.

John Davis

John Davis was heavy weight champ of the world when he was seventeen and won a few more meets before he was in the service in the Pacific Theater in World War II. He got malaria there and it took a while for him to recover. When he got out of the service he started training again. He was in the Los Angele area for a while and he came over and trained with us. John had very small hands in spite of being over 6'1". And it was hard for him to grip the bar. What he did to strengthen his hands for gripping the bar was pick up two 45 pound plates, smooth side, and hold them straight out for ten seconds in each hand.

Paul Anderson, "The Dixie Derrick" and Jimmy Lee

Paul Anderson, "The Dixie Derrick," trained with us two times. Paul squatted 800 pounds 20 times. That was all we could put on the bar! Paul won the Olympics in 1956. He was six feet tall and weighed 370 pounds. He was fast and powerful. At those same Olympics Paul finished only one step behind Jimmy Lee in the 40 yard dash. Jimmy won the 400 meter Olympic Championship. Paul vertical jumped 34"!

Dave Sheppard

Dave Sheppard, who placed second at two Olympic Games weighing 198 and 220, trained a lot with us. He used to bring a half gallon of beer and drink it during our workout. At the Olympic tryouts he barely missed a world record snatch of 316. He lost his balance. Well, he had been sipping Hill and Hill whiskey before he lifted. Enough said.

Arkady Vorobiev

The World record was held by Arkady Vorobiev (Arkady Nikitich Vorobyov) of the USSR in the snatch at 314 pounds. He was also a medical doctor. And while most of the lifters in the world were using the squat style in this lift, he used the split.

Pete George, Squat Style of Lifting

The squat style was developed by Pete George of Akron, Ohio. He had a famous coach, Larry Barnholth. Larry started his lifters using the squat style because the ceiling of Larry's garage, where they lifted, was too low to use the split style. Pete placed second to Frank Spellman at the 1948 Olympics as I said earlier and then went on to win two other Olympic Games.

Chuck Vinci

In the 1950s the USA had a bantamweight lifter, Chuck Vinci. At 123 pounds, Chuck was a fierce competitor against Vladimir Stogov of the USSR. Chuck won two Olympic Games. One year at the World Championships he tried to beat Stogov's world record in the clean and jerk of 292. In each lift, the lifter had three attempts. In those days the lifter could make a fourth attempt, but if successful, it wouldn't count toward his total. Well, Chuck tried 294 on the fourth, fifth, sixth, seventh, eighth and ninth attempts—missing each time. One can imagine how tired he was. Peter George, his teammate, urged him to make a tenth attempt, but Chuck said he was too tired. Pete responded, "The world record is held by Stogov of USSR and they don't believe in God. You are a good Catholic, right Chuck?" Chuck said, "Yes." So on his tenth attempt, he clean and jerked 294 successfully for new a world record. This was the first time anybody had set a world record on his tenth attempt. In fact, nobody ever lifted a world record on a fifth attempt. Today in competition, a world Record has to be achieved in one of three attempts.

UCLA and UC Berkley

My path to UCLA was a bit unusual. On the weekends I used to earn money doing lawns, shrubs and trees. At one time my good friend Tony Fantuzoto planned to take the entrance exams to UCLA which were offered on a Saturday. I told him I couldn't take the exams because of my weekend jobs. Well, it rained that Saturday, so I had the day off, took the test and passed. I didn't really know what my path would be, so I asked Tony what he was going to major in. He said "pre-dental," and so I did pre-dental too.

In college my main sport was Olympic-style lifting and I continued to train with Frank Spellman. I also played one year as quarterback for the UCLA Bruins. After a while, it dawned on me that I shouldn't play quarterback because there were simply others with more talent. I wisely dropped football and focused on weightlifting.

When I was twenty, after training with Frank since the age of fourteen, I told Tony I enjoyed the sciences required for pre-dental but I didn't want to go into it because I didn't want to be looking down people's mouths the rest of my life. I then transferred to UC Berkeley and majored in exercise physiology and Tony transferred to USC and majored in pharmacy. At the time of this writing, Tony still owns a pharmacy on Atlantic Boulevard in Long Beach. While at Berkley I continued weightlifting and added javelin, discus and boxing. Some great track and field athletes trained with us from time to time: Dave Davis, Beary O'Brian, Jay Syvester and Dallas Long.

National Weightlifting Championships and Clarence Bass

In 1961 the national collegiate weightlifting championships were to be held at the University of Maryland. At the age of seventeen I wanted to participate so badly that I sold the beloved MG I had for a plane ticket and I loved it. I only placed fourth but set a national teen-age record in the snatch at 255 pounds. I went with Kurt Freeman, a training partner and San Francisco policeman. He was in my class and placed second. We met many people, lifters, University of Maryland students and professors and enjoyed the city of Baltimore. This experience made such a positive impression on me that I continued to lift and to progress. The next year, I couldn't compete because I had injured myself throwing the javelin.

Most importantly, while at the national teen-age weightlifting championships, I met Clarence Bass, who took second. I told him that was the last time he was going to beat me. That was because he remained in the 165 pound class and I moved to the 181 and 198 pound classes. As a result, we never competed against one another again. We continued to meet over the years, becoming very good friends. Clarence became famous for winning the past forty Mr. America contest, writing many, many books on physical fitness and weight training and today he has many clients from all over the world going to Albuquerque to seek his knowledge on this and nutrition. He is teamed with his wife Carol in reaching many people on these topics and more.

Two years after selling the MG I bought a 1947 Dodge. This was the year I competed in the national collegiate championships at the University of Montana in Bozman. At the age of 19 I won in the 198 pound class. In those days, Olympic weightlifting was a club sport, not a university sanctioned sport, so we had to pay for all our expenses, as we did when we went to the University of Maryland. We raised money by going out into the community asking for support. Learning to fend for ourselves was a great experience for college students. We had a sponsor, Cap Pease, and he drove us there, along with Pete Carlton, a graduate English major and Dav Maggard, who played two years varsity football at Cal, qualified and went to the 1968 Olympic Games in Mexico City. We all won first place and our team placed second. Bozeman was home to Gene Fulmar, former middle weight world champion. It was a big moment for us as we got to meet him and have lunch with him.

I love Olympic-style weightlifting. I snatched 281 pounds and clean and jerked 325 pounds in New Orleans in 1979 when I was 39 years old. These remain my best marks. At the age of 60 I set a Masters record of 260 in the snatch in Budagers, New Mexico.

Boxing and Coach Edgar Nemir

In college I learned boxing from coach Ed Nemir. It was a methods class. I boxed for two years in 1961 and 1962 and had two 5-4 records. So you can see I wasn't great, but I learned about the sport through competing and from coach Nemir. He toured the country successfully in wrestling and boxing while also earning a law degree. He went into law to please his mother. When he earned his degree, he put it on her desk because he thought she deserved it and then taught for many years at

Cal as the boxing and wrestling coach. He died during a coaching session with his son who was boxing for Cal.

At the University of California, boxing was a big activity. There were only about five schools in the nation that had boxing at that time. Many schools had dropped it because of injuries and even death. Boxing teams had former service men who gained a lot of boxing experience while in the service. They were much advanced over other college students on the team who had started with no experience. In my twenty years of teaching boxing in schools and recreation centers, we had no injuries.

Classmates who became Olympians

In a practice for the 40 yard dash, I finished 1/10 second behind Willy White. Willy went on to compete in the 1964 Olympics. I asked Willy who would win and he said, "He who is the hungriest." I mention this, because Willy had made the 1964 Olympic team. I had three other classmates who made the Olympics: David Maggard, Jack Yearman, and Jerry Seabert.

In the 1964 Olympics, Peter Snell, from New Zealand took first place in the 800 meter. Jerry said Peter was absolutely amazing with such stamina. There were three heats and one could keep up with Snell for the first two heats, but in the third heat Snell blew everyone away. Snell had all the wins and publicity leading up to the Olympics

Berkeley Coach Brutus Hamilton

At the University of California at Berkeley I went out for discus and javelin, as I've said. There my coach was the legendary Brutus Hamilton. He brought out the best in his athletes by getting them ready through proper peaking. His rival coach was Payton Jorn at Stanford. Payton would really get his athletes up but he over trained them. Brutus would say Stanford did too much psyching up and then they wouldn't give a top performance.

President Ronald Reagan and First Lady Nancy Reagan

Ronald and Nancy Regan brought to me, and probably many others—costiveness, the can do attitude. There have been many leaders and the one thing that they bring to their flock is to believe they can do what they say they will do. Positiveness can be harmful also. Hitler united Germany because the Germans believed what he said and in their race superiority. Just an example of how some good things can be used in harmful ways.

President Richard Nixon

To me, President Nixon brought a comeback attitude. Think of all the people against him. And at the depths he made a comeback which was to me unbelievable. He wrote some great books after his fallen presidency. World leaders sought his advice. But he did have those faults we all remember.

Red Grange and George Halas

Red Grange, "The Galloping Ghost," made seven touchdowns in one game at the University of Illinois. When George Halas started the NFL his number one pick for the Chicago Bears was Red Grange. He made the NFL with his running ability and his gentle manners were legendary. He and George Halas swam together at lunch with my dad at the Chicago Athletic Club. Like my dad, George Halas believed strongly in keeping in shape. He used to come to our house about once a week. I remember him throwing me many passes and once I came off cut for a pass and tripped over the sidewalk. My dad said, "Hell, he fell." Red said, "Don't worry that he fell, let's see how he gets up." Being told that by this great NFL star always stuck with me. I fell many times in the sports I played and Red's voice always went through my head and I always got up, never quit.

Walt Becker

Walt Becker was the father of a girl I was dating at one time when I was young. We used to train together when I wasn't able to train at Frank Spellman's garage. Walt was a truant officer in the Los Angeles school district. He took me around his beat many times. He wanted to show me how bad the kids were that he worked with. We went to their schools and homes. These were tough guys. I got to know them, their neighborhoods, their parents, their siblings. Walt explained that to influence these kids you had to earn their trust and show them you really care. What he did was get into these boys where they lived and spend time with them. This really seemed to open them up. Walt used athletics as a way to relate. Many a time we went to the Los Angeles Coliseum to play football, do track and field, boxing and wrestling. He let the boys use the team's shower facilities. He had such a jovial manner that he was able to convince local businesses to donate athletic equipment, food, milk, soft drinks, sports magazines and books. He also recruited local adults to work with our boys.

When he was criticized by his bosses for spending too much time with these "street urchins," he pointed out the drop in gang and street violence. The local businesses raved about Walt's work. Eventually the kids started to teach each other. Walt talked with the kids about setting goals and he talked to them in a way that made sense to them—straight talk, no B.S. His daughter (whom I was dating) brought in some fellow female sport teammates. This allowed the boys to see that girls could be exceptional in sports and it opened their eyes to thinking of girls in ways they hadn't even thought of before.

My relationship with Walt actually grew even after his daughter and I broke up and he became a great father figure to me.

Internship at the University of Arizona

In 1962 and 1963 I had an internship at the University of Arizona at Tucson for graduate school. There was a lot to learn in exercise physiology. The staff there were as good as those at UC Berkeley. I received my masters there and was fortunate to be able to attend the University of Arizona on an academic scholarship. This university had been called the playground of the south, but when I got there, there was no more of that and they had five new, young professors in exercise physiology and biomechanics.

I met up with two great athletes, Joe Crider an all America quarterback from Colorado State and Rory Weber, national heavyweight wrestling champ from Northwestern. We rented an apartment together and learned from each other for two years. In our last two months, Weber had to return to Chicago as his dad was dying. Joe and I could not then afford the rent so we slept and ate at the university football stadium. The janitor there thought our wives had kicked us out of the house! Money was really tight. I ate on a dollar and a half a day—one pound of hamburger, one quart of milk and a Payday candy bar. Under the terms of my scholarship, I was required to teach wrestling. However, I knew nothing about it, so I had to get resourceful. I took Rory's wrestling class in the morning and then I taught the same thing to the freshman in the afternoon!

3

Peace Corps in South America, 1963–1965

Both my father and stepfather served in WWII and I badly wanted to serve my country in the military also, but President Johnson and Congress had passed a bill which said that if you were married they wouldn't allow you to serve. I had gotten married, so Lynn, my wife at the time, and I applied to the Peace Corps and went through three months of training at the University of Arizona where I had just graduated. Also at our training was Sargent Shriver (husband of Eunice Kennedy) and his daughter Maria, who went on to become a TV personality and later was married for a time to Arnold Schwarzenegger.

After three months of learning the language (five hours a day), history and customs of Colombia, we were sent to Cali, the sports capital of Colombia. They wanted coaches to train their best athletes so they could win in international competition. Besides myself, the Colombians also invited coaches from Japan, USSR, Romania, England, France, Spain, Bulgaria and Germany. What a great learning and cultural learning experience. While there, I travelled around South America on athletic trips and when Lynn and I were on vacation. We didn't go to Venezuela because it and Colombia didn't like each other. We saw great people, sportsmen and beautiful landscapes on our travels.

Finding A Place To Live

The altitude in Cali is about 5,000 feet. Upon arrival, we walked the streets looking for a place to live. Interestingly, a couple from Spain, Lorenzo and Josefina Cabrara in their late sixties, who had immigrated to Santo Domingo, and then to Colombia during the Spanish Civil War asked us what we were doing walking the streets. We told them and they said they had a big house with an extra room and they were willing to rent it out to us. This was really convenient because the stadium where I mainly worked was in walking distance as was the hospital where Lynn did physical therapy. We lived two wonderful years with them. We usually ate breakfast and dinner with them and cleaned up after ourselves and helped with general work around the house. Many times we played Chinese checkers at night and it was Spain (Lorenzo) against Santo Domingo (Josephina), and against us. The neighbors were great and we played with the kids in the neighborhood. There was a street vendor who came every morning selling bread with cheeses.

Lorenzo and Josefina were wonderful people I learned a lot about the Spanish Civil War and Europe and we talked many times about the US role in Vietnam. They thought it was not in our best interest to be there. We also talked a lot about Colombia's government, its relations with its neighbors and the Colombian people.

We met many Colombians and socialized with them. They really liked parties and the national drink was liquorice flavored called Aguardiente. We didn't drink alcohol, so only sipped it from time to time. There was lots of dancing at the parties—usually the Cumbia, their national dance. Very much done to a Latin beat. Sometimes the parties were on the beach which I liked a lot—the water going around my feet and legs and the water was warm.

Eliseo Carrasco

Eliseo Carrasco was our leader. So low key yet very intense. But I was also intense and stepped on many toes. Finally so much so that Eliseo asked me if I wanted to be sent home. I sure didn't and he told me to be less volatile or he would. I calmed down and had many successes, including the eight year old record miler, Pthen Pedro Grajales and Alvardo Mejia who made the Tokyo Olympics and did well and Ney Lopez middle-weight lift, and Hiram Lozano who later became the Olympic Weightlifting coach in the 1976 Olympics.

The Stadium Where We Trained

The stadium where most of the sports were practiced was one and a half miles away—a really good walk. We had a weight room in the stadium with a few rats running around, but with all our activity they soon went into hiding. The weight lifting was geared to the track events each kid was doing. There I helped coach their national weightlifting team with their great coach and competitor, Ney Lopez. I learned much from Ney. I weight trained their national track and field team, swimming team and soccer team.

Training Successes

In Colombia, as I said, I weight trained 200 meter Champion Pedro Grajales and long distance runner Alvaro Mejia. Both were mature athletes in their late twenties and I knew they didn't use steroids. The weight training helped Pedro make the 200 meter qualifying time for the upcoming Tokyo Olympics. Before I trained him, he was 3/10 off the qualifying time. He was 29 and hadn't made progress in three years. His coach Carlos Avila wanted to weight train him to see if he could qualify. After only three months of weight training, he did qualify! We were all ecstatic.

Alvaro Mejia, in those three months, took off eight seconds from his 10,000 meter time to easily qualify for the 1964 Tokyo Olympics.

During this time I weight trained eight year old Jaimi Escalante, who set a world record in the 5,000 meter for his age and was featured in *Sports illustrated*.

We also trained Benjamin Alvarez, an eight year old who ran a world record in the mile and was also featured in *Sports Illustrated*.

Another runner, Guiyermo Sanches, was ten seconds away from qualifying for the Tokyo Olympics in the 5,000 meters. After weight training with me, he qualified 15 seconds under the time needed. So close.

I weight trained the swimmers and the soccer team and although they improved greatly it wasn't enough to go to the Olympics. Nevertheless, all the swimmers qualified for the Pan American Championships and the Colombian soccer team made the South American Championships.

A lifter I trained for almost the whole two years I was in Colombia, Hernan Aguirre was just off the South American record in the snatch. Before I left Colombia I told him that he must break that record. To do that, there would be no more drinking and nightly carousing with girls. Then I broke the head of a beer bottle over the railing of the outside bar. I held the jagged edge under his chin and I said "You're going to do it for yourself, your family, your country and most of all for me, who has to put up with all your garbage for two years." I don't know whether he followed what I told him, but he did break that record in the next competition. Interesting what a little threat will do.

My lifter Ney Lopez, who placed tenth in the World Weightlifting Championships in Stockholm, Sweden also qualified for the same Olympics as did my lifter Hernan Aquirre.

I could go on and on. The improvement in these athletes was noticed by the coaches of the Japanese world class women's volleyball team and the Japanese baseball team, the Honque Braves. Both of those organizations offered me jobs training their athletes. The University of Valle exercise department offered me a job doing research in the weight training of different athletes. Accepting this type of work was a dream come true.

National Institute of Physical Education

In the two years I was in Cali weight training their national team and individuals, I also taught exercise physiology at the National Institute of Physical Education in Bogota. I would fly out on a Friday and return Sunday night after teaching. In the Peace Corps orientation we were told that Aviana Airlines did not have a good safety record, but it was the only airline flying, so I flew a lot on Aviana from a town called Thagua to Cali via Bogota. I remember walking up the steps of the old DC 3, then walking up the slant of the inside of the plane to my seat. Eventually they turned on those little fans. They always filled me with a feeling of apprehension in this relic of a plane! Besides teaching, I learned a lot about exercise physiology. They were really up to date. I found Bogota to be more formal than Cali.

I once visited an emerald mine and a gold mine outside Bogota. Smuggling emeralds out of the country was a big problem (this was before drug smuggling). Every once in a while the paper would have an article about the police shooting an emerald smuggler. This was a tame event compared to the drug smuggling of later years.

Panela

Before leaving Colombia I did research on a sugar extract called panela. I found out that panela had many vitamins and minerals. I single out panela because athletes were eating it in small bite sized pieces. They liked it with lemon and hot water—agua panela con limon. Coaches thought it was a waste. It had one interesting problem: when it was diluted in water it fermented quickly. One day I had glasses of panela fermenting in the sun. A good glass of this fermentation would make one inebriated quickly. The athletes thought this was fun. Their coaches didn't. So we were careful in the fermentation process. We liked adding lemon to it so the athletes I worked with had agua panela con limon on a regular basis.

Boys on the Streets

I wanted to help the little street boys who might have been home-less or from very poor families and who were ever-present. I knew the stadium where all the athletic teams trained was vacant from twelve to two in the afternoon. I asked some of the businesses if they would be willing to hire the boys if I trained them in some simple skills which could be used in the stores. They agreed so for two years I used track and field, soccer, Olympic-style weight lifting and boxing as a medium to reach these kids. They were trained to be on time, how to stock materials and how to be polite and courteous to customers. I even got a milk company to deliver daily cartons of milk and they were allowed to use the stadium showers. What a good time we had! Each group was made up of six to eight boys and each group went from six to eight weeks. In the two years I was there we trained twelve groups and the businesses hired about forty boys.

Once when a couple of my kids were weight training under the stadium, one asked the other to pass the weightlifting bar. The kid with the bar just threw it at him and the bar landed on his toe and split it in two. I thought it was going to drop off. The stadium was only a half mile from the hospital. I picked the kid up in my arms and got there as fast as I could but there was no doctor on duty and I could only find an intern. We took the kid into a room and there was enough connection of the toe that the intern could stitch the toe together. He told the kid to come back in five days so he could change the dressing. Well, the kid didn't come back in five days so I went to his house. I reminded him and told his parents that the dressing had to be changed. It was so dirty I thought he might already have an infection. He was wearing no shoes. This went on and on and after about three weeks I couldn't find him at his house. His parents didn't know where he was. I didn't see him for quite a while. He finally came by the stadium and wanted to start lifting again. He was wearing the same dressing and this time it was black and dirty with street garbage. I took him to his home and again told his parents that he could lose his foot due to infection. Every week for six weeks I went to his house and one time his parents said they hadn't seen him for a month. I gave up. I finally saw him after about six months. The bandage was off and the foot and toe looked good. He must have been immune to just about everything!

Snakes on the Road to New Buena Ventura

One of the trips our athletes made was to a small village near the north east of New Buena Ventura, a big fishing port. On our way to the village, our cars ran over several snakes slithering out of the dense jungle. The snakes were two to four feet long. At one point we got a flat tire. My job was to keep the snakes away with a stick or by throwing rocks at them while the bus driver changed the tire. Some of the snakes were poisonous. This was successful and reaching the village at dusk, the locals told us to burn candles at night to keep away both snakes and rats. This was good advice. We slept in a big tent with a roof of leaf branches supported by wooden beams. We heard the rats rattling around in the roof all night long, but thankfully they didn't come near us because of the candles.

The village had about two hundred people, all very nice. They farmed, hunted in the jungle for meat and raised sheep. I and seven other trainers were there for a few weeks and they fed us a lot of beans and rice and plenty of soups. In this village they practiced the two sports we were to teach: Olympic-style lifting and volleyball to the teenagers in an opened frame building. Although at the time there were no international competitions for women, they said they wanted to be prepared. The Peace Corps paid for part of this training and they paid for part. About thirty kids enthusiastically participated.

They were sorry to see us go. We had fun together working on a common goal of weight lifting and volleyball. This was the first such camp the Peace Corps tried. After our success, other groups ventured out.

Cheeseburgers In Bogota

When traveling around the country, we liked to go to Bogota, the capital of Colombia, to get a good meal. On one trip we got there late and the only business open was an outdoor hamburger place. We ordered cheeseburgers and while waiting we saw rats above us on the rafters. The cheeseburgers came with more than we bargained for—worm larva in the cheese! Later we took a plane to Cali and had some good food with no rats or maggots.

Torture in the Chemistry Lab

While in Bogota for a week long conference in athletics, I would go to the track at lunchtime and jog three or four miles. On one Thursday I was out jogging when I saw four men in suits running behind me. I thought that was strange—men jogging in suits. They looked like guys who knew how to get things done. Before I knew it, they up and grabbed me and hustled me off to the chemistry lab at the university. This scared the hell out of me. They wanted me to sign a statement that the Peace Corps was an affiliate of the FBI and CIA. When I refused they heated some metal rods over a Bunsen burner and said they would burn my eyes out and scar my penis if I didn't cooperate. I told them that the Peace Corps had a great reputation in Colombia and harming me would cause them to lose favor with the people. At that time, Colombia had the most Peace Corps volunteers in the world—500 in total. It took all the fortitude I could muster not to cry out. After about a half hour they stopped torturing me and let me go, instructing me not to tell anyone about what happened and I never did—no one ever knew. I was left with two scars—one in the corner of my eye and the other on the side of my penis. I still have one of the propaganda posters of theirs that said the Peace Corps was an agent of the CIA.

It turns out that the men who captured and tortured me were guerillas from the hills left over from the terrible civil war called The Bogotasa in 1948. After the civil war, the government implemented a plan in which the liberals would be in control for four years, followed by the conservatives in control. From time to time the guerillas would try and frighten the government. When they took me to the lab that day they were mad because during that time President Johnson had sent twenty-five thousand troops to Santo Domingo to prevent it from going communist.

The Colombian Mindset

In Colombian, if a certain plan didn't work, they would quickly abandon it and go to a new plan. In other words, they felt that the original must be a bad plan. We were told right when we arrived that the follow through was lacking—it was not necessarily the plan that was bad, but the willingness to work the plan that was at fault. The mindset of not following through meant they were not going to spend the time on anything that took a lot of effort. The mindset was, when difficulties come up, just get a new plan! It was plain that the Colombians just had to work together and be patient with the plans and with themselves.

Food there was tasty and varied. One of the main foods was a sort of soup called zancocho. It was a national dish and we used this as an example of how you could work through problems to achieve perfection, like the soup. I used this as an example of how time and effort gives a good result. I also used the method of washing clothes as an example of involvement. Many of the clothes were washed in the river or ponds. They recognized the problem of pollution and that it took a lot of time. So the market grew for washers and dryers. Refrigerators the same thing. Use and ownership of refrigerators went up strikingly during the two years I was there. So there was progress and accomplishments that were tangible.

In Colombia the people were always slow to get things done. I called it the land of next week.

After I left, drug trafficking got worldwide attention. And, as played up in the press, the big place was Medellin and the Medellin Cartel. I thought, sure if you wanted things done and done well, you went to Medellin. As an aside, after WWII many Germans immigrated to Medellin. It had a totally different mindset than the rest of the country. Ideas flourished there and goods moved.

In many cases Colombia was advanced in making things, but slow in promoting and getting them to market. And this needed many people working together. They said sports was a good way to show this. One could readily see this in their team sports of soccer and basketball. But it was in their culture to not work together well. Team sports needed cooperation and individual sports needed it to stage competitions. So getting players to work together was a big priority for us. We wanted to introduce the concept of working together in sports as an example for government or business. To develop this required cooperation between individuals. It was stated that outside of their families people just didn't work well together and it was vital to break this custom. Sports are a great way to foster this. It is very important to learn cooperation in this way so that it becomes part of the learning experience for young people.

Once during a basketball game two players on the same team started fighting and that left just three players actively playing against the other team of five players. In soccer I also saw players fighting amongst themselves. The other players just played on. We were told about this behavior in training but it was a real shock to see it carried out!

In contrast, the Japanese did great things in sports together. And a lot of this was due to cooperation. But then individual initiative might be less and individual creativity might not happen. So in general, I would say I experienced in Japan a focus on perfecting something, but brand new ideas were difficult to implement. In basketball, for example, the Japanese would have a game plan and they stuck to it. When we played against them and changed it up—throwing in new moves—they had a hard time adjusting. They could do it but didn't have the experience or cultural training to strike out on their own.

Venezuela

When in Colombia, one of the first places I considered taking the Colombian weight lifting team to was the neighboring country of Venezuela. However, every member of the team vehemently opposed this because they did not like the Venezuelans as I said earlier. I wanted to go there very much so I asked our lifters if they had ever met a Venezuelan. They said they hadn't and I replied "Well, maybe if you met them you might like them." They said, "No, they would hate them more." The hatred seems to go back to a border war which took place many years ago. The feeling was so strong that I dropped the idea. So, we started our competitive tour going the other way—starting with Ecuador.

Ecuador

We started from the coast city of Guayaquil and took a train to the capital city of Quito. The train went through five climate zones—the most variety in climates experienced in one trip than any other trip in the world. It was very striking to experience this. So much change in a relatively short distance. During the ride, vendors would come every so often selling everything from fruits to meats. Lamb was the specialty but everything was delicious.

The people (mainly Ecuadorian) were very friendly and seemed happy. The political situation was stable then, but Ecuador had more presidents than the number of years it was independent from Spain.

The competition we staged in Ecuador was surprisingly close and we won. Here is another country in which the government wanted to do well in international competition and they provided many of the athletic teams with equipment, paid for room and board, and covered travel costs to hold competitions. The atmosphere was fun and the host team took us around to show us the sites and the people who were very kind to us.

Bolivia and Chile

The Bolivians in the past had fought a hard war against the Chileans. The Chileans took away Bolivia's only coastal sea town, Arica, but they are now good neighbors. I did work in Cali with some Bolivians. They wanted to talk about the USA's past with Native Americans. They thought it was terrible that the USA put them on reservations. I replied that they (Bolivian's) didn't put their Native Americans on reservations—that they shot most of them. That ended that conversation.

I never went to Bolivia for athletic competition, but I did go there on part of a vacation trip. I remember going down into La Paz, the capital. We were following a truck full of military soldiers. It was an open truck and they all were having fun pointing guns at us, but nothing happened. I say "down," but La Paz was still high up at about 12,000 feet. And it was there that the news came over that one of our space crafts blew up, killing all on board. The people were very sympathetic to us as they admired our space program. I didn't expect this as Bolivia was a very mountainous country with a very unstable political history. It had about as many presidents as did Ecuador following its independence from Spain. The people seemed happy in spite of this and in spite of having no seaport—further isolating it from the world.

From Bolivia we flew to Santiago, Chile, a very beautiful city with the wonderful seaport of Valparaiso. We visited a Chilean friend who had been a patient at the hospital where my wife worked in Cali, Colombia. I remember vividly the many dances they loved to do. One was the Cueca, where the woman strung out a bandana across her hips. It was very intricate and colorful—not risqué.

Crossing over the Andes was scary as the Cordillera Mountains were quite high and snow bound. And to top it off, we were flying on Aviana airlines, which I mentioned earlier. I recall a book called *Alive* written about an Aviana crash in which five passengers survived the crash and walked out of the mountains to a small town where they were cared for. They eventually went on to write that book.

Argentina

Argentina back then was a hot bed of Olympic weightlifting. A super heavy weight named Humberto Selvetti tied with the American hero Paul Anderson in the Melbourne, Australia Olympic Games. Although they tied, Paul Anderson won the gold medal because he weighed less than Selvetti. Both were over 300 pounds. It was a big surprise. Paul had lifted considerably more than any man and many of his records remain unbeaten. Even at his body weight, he had a vertical jump of 38 inches high—as high as NBA Basketball players. He also finished only one step behind Jimmy Lea in a 40 yard race. Lea at that time had the world record in the 400 meters and was Olympic Champion at that distance.

Argentina was a big beef producing country and Selvetti was called the "bull of the pampas." The pampas were huge land plains where cattle grazed.

Uraguay and Brazil

We also went to Uraguay, then Brazil. Beautiful countries and friendly people. Their big sport was soccer, made famous later by the Brazilian player Pele. Pele brought soccer to the attention of sports fans in the USA. He was the greatest soccer player in the world and very charismatic.

Thoughts On Discrimination

As I worked in the Peace Corps in Colombia, I learned a lot about various peoples' discrimination. We often think only in terms of our own discrimination at home. Traveling around in South America and Asia and when I worked in Japan I learned about theirs. Unfortunately, it seems that this is world wide. It is no good and it is important to fight against it and to realize that no country or people have a monopoly on discrimination or on goodness.

USA is the Greatest Country

My being an Olympic coach for the USA has taken me to many countries behind the old iron curtain. I learned much about these other cultures and I like to feel that the USA is the greatest country in world. Our constitution and bill of rights are really great documents. It is just amazing that they were ever written. We have endured many ups and downs but always keep going forward and getting better. I keep a positive attitude.

Revolution

Colombia once had a huge revolution and it left the country at bitter odds with itself. There were deep animosities between people and neighborhoods—liberals against conservatives. Each side had guns stored up expecting the war to come. Guns were stashed everywhere, including in statues of Mary and Christ.

A popular liberal leader, Jorge Eliécer Gaitán, was murdered in the streets of Bogota resulting in violent rioting and looting in the streets and referred to as "The Bogotazo" or the "Bogota attack." This started almost fifteen years of intense bloodshed, referred to as "La Violencia." When we arrived, what remained were guerrillas fighting the public and each other. They were not political ideologues. It was hard to understand that these good people could have had a national war that tore the country apart for years.

As I said before, what Colombia did was set up a presidency of alternating beliefs—four years of liberal and then four years of conservatism and this was done twice. And after this there to be free elections. It seemed to work. We were there during the second rotation.

Bus To Ibague

There were bloody guerilla attacks from time to time. For example, I was to give a sports clinic in Ibague, a city between Bogota and Cali. I flew to Bogota then took a bus to Ibague. Going from Ibague was dangerous, we were told, as this was where the guerillas were at their strongest.

In the bus from Bogota to Ibague we rounded a big hill and suddenly all hell broke loose. I had never heard gunshot but I heard this pop pop pop. And a window in the bus came crashing down. My Colombia partner and I were at the back of the bus. The back of the bus had two doors so we quickly opened them, jumped out, and ran to the hills. For over two hours we heard gun shots and moans and groans from the bus. When the gun shots finally stopped we slowly came down and approached the scene. The guerillas were gone but there was a sickening sight in the bus—young kids, babies, mothers, fathers, grandparents all hacked up—probably by machetes.

There was nothing we could do so we then walked many hours to Ibague. We told the elders what had happened first and then the rest of population. The people were grief stricken and so were we. It turns out we couldn't walk or drive to Cali at that time because the roads were not safe from guerillas. So we slept over in Ibague and an armored car from Bogota came and we climbed in and went to Bogota. From there we waited hours to fly back to Cali. When we arrived we were given clean clothes, got washed up, and were told to say nothing of what happened.

In two days we were taken by planes to Washington DC to give them the full report. Because of the delicacy of the Peace Corps in various countries, Peace Corps Washington wanted no press on this. We were told that such things happened in other countries and in some cases when word got out the host country got embarrassed as well as the Peace Corps. You've got to remember the Peace Corps was only two years old and things like this could endanger the young program.

We were not to tell our wives, girlfriends, or friends. Nobody, nobody, nobody.

Bull Fighting

Back when I was still in the Peace Corps, I remember that I had always wanted to learn how to fight bulls. It was not my intent to become a bullfighter but to learn how to do the various moves. I agreed to train my bullfighting trainer in Olympic weightlifting if he would train me in bullfighting. So he took me to a small corral with a small bull without horns. He then taught me how to make passes with the bull and had me

72

practice these moves for three weeks. At the end of that time he told me to have the bull make a pass at me and then to drop the cape and walk away. It was scary because I had not developed any real skill at this and the bull was big, muscular and quick. I asked, "What if the bull charges?" "He won't," assured the trainer. So I made a pass with the bull and took about five or six steps away. But after a couple of steps I could hear him coming and it was too late. He hit me in the mid to low back. It knocked my breath away and I went down. I rolled over, trying to keep the bull away, but he kept driving his head into my shoulders and snorting. He was really mad. It terrified me so I put my hands on his head to try to keep him away but he kept driving his head into my shoulder. The trainer and other people on horses used short capes and yelled at the bull and whistled. Finally the bull was under control and they helped me up and took me to a nearby hospital.

I was really hurting but could walk and move my arms. My back was very stiff and sore. I was examined for a long time and x-rays were taken. I was told my whole lumbar area was damaged but they said it would heal by itself with time. Boy were they wrong! My right shoulder had also been dislocated and the clavicle and humerus were broken but still in place. The left shoulder was okay. I was then told that eventually my back would have to be fused and my shoulders fixed too. So much for healing by itself. After three weeks I was released from the hospital and continued my work with the athletes. I was given a brace for my back to ease the pain and my shoulder was put in a brace to restrict motion.

Meanwhile, in the early summer of 1964, the Japanese women's volleyball team called Nichibo came to Cali. They put on a demonstration showing how they trained. They had heard that I had increased the vertical jump and speed of Colombian team and field athletes through Olympic weightlifting. They thought this might work with their volleyball team. The Europeans had an edge in height so it was important for the Japanese girls to be faster and jump higher.

Before long the officials for the Japanese approached me to train the team in vertical jump and speed. I asked about hours and money and about any other possibilities. They said they would have to talk to the Hanku Braves and officials at Mikage University. After their tour I was told that they wanted me and sent me a contract spelling out my duties for two or three years. It was a good schedule with excellent opportunities. So even though I was in a lot of pain, I finished out my Peace Corps stint in Colombia and went to Japan. The pain got very intense, so I eventually had back surgery in Japan and again in Chicago as a result of this injury. I will discuss these surgeries later in the book.

Leaving Colombia

Before I leave my thoughts on the Peace Corps, in 1965, a few weeks before we were to leave Colombia each in our group was given a Peace Corps syllabus with lots of pictures on the progress made and how the Colombians had benefited from our working with them.

One was picture of a big watering storage tank for the people in the barrio of Siloe. Another was a big picture of the water diversion system in downtown Cali. I had never seen them. Siloe certainly need water storage tank and downtown Cali needed a diversion system because when it rained down town Cali really flooded. But these two projects were not even started, let alone finished. This felt to us as if the pictures and the descriptions of the projects were some kind of propaganda. Maybe those two projects were completed later, but not by us. Others in our group who were going on home said similar things like this had taken place where they lived in Colombia. We tried to get appointments with the US Ambassador, but with no success.

So we just left and headed for Japan.

I just gotta find
that Delsey –
it's soft like Kleenex!

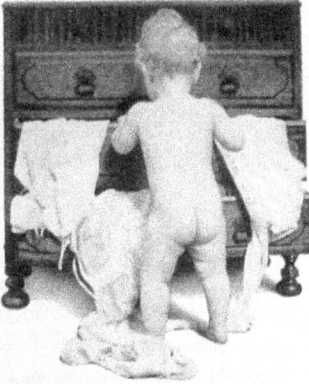

DELSEY* TOILET PAPER
soft like Kleenex*
tissues; double-ply
for extra strength

3 rolls for 25¢
12 rolls for 97¢

"I just gotta find that Delsey...it's soft like Kleenex!" Carl was one year old in Chicago when the Delsey toilet tissue company had him pose for this photograph used in their advertising campaign.

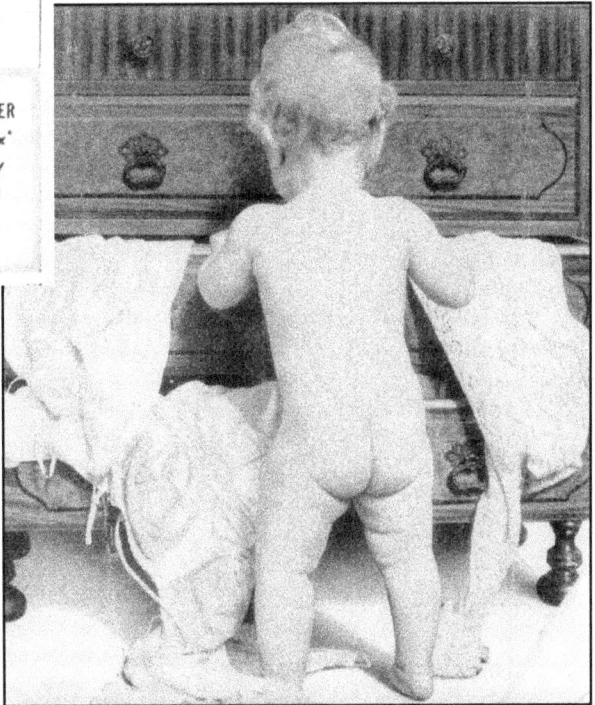

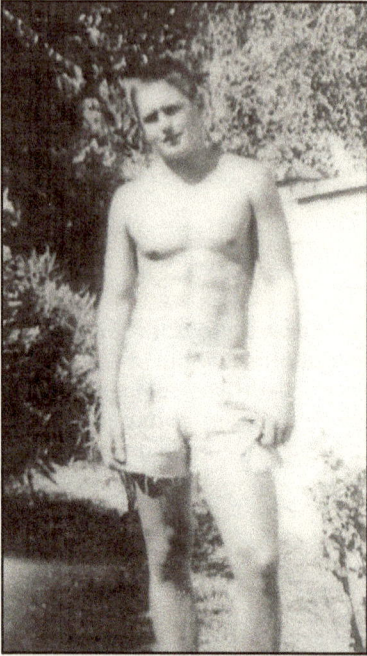

Carl at thirteen in Los Angeles.

Carl with Red Grange, 1952, in Chicago. Grange was known as the Galloping Ghost because he had scored seven touchdowns in one game.

Carl's dad, Jerry, just back from the 1948 Olympic Games in London where he competed in water polo. He also participated in the same sport in the 1936 Olympics in Berlin.

Carl in 1962 with stepmother Marilyn and father Jerry.

To CARL WITH BEST WISHES FRANK SPELLMAN (264 ON BAR)

Frank Spellman, 1948 Olympic champion. Carl met him at the Bert Goodrich gym in 1952 and was invited to train with him in his garage. Carl trained with him eight years and was like a father to him.

Carl with Jaime Rojas (left), Ney Lopez, Herman Aguire, and Hiram Lozano. All were South American champions. Ney Lopez placed seventh at the weightlifting World Championships in Stockholm in 1963. Hiram went on to become the Olympic coach for Colombia in the 1976 Olympics in Montreal.

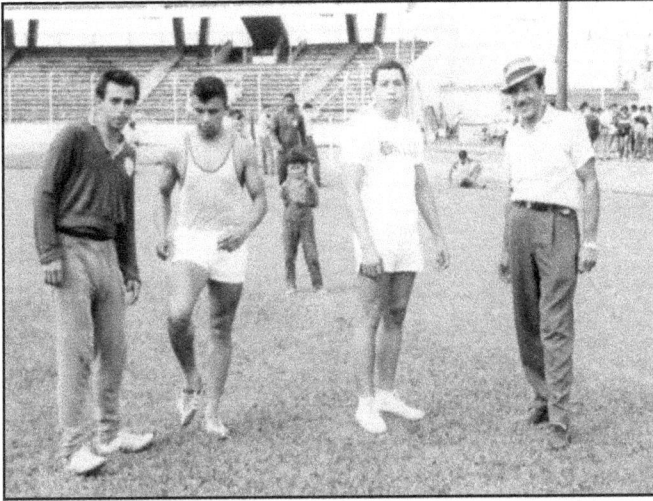

In Colombia, Pedro Gonzales (far left) and coach Carlos
Avila (far right). Pedro Gonzales made the 1964 and 1968
Olympic Games placing fourth each time in the 200 and
400 meter races. Carlos Avila was Colombian National and
Olympic track coach during the same years.

Carl Miller, the "Peace Corps Years"

Circa 1967

ALWAYS THE INNOVATOR, CARL BROUGHT TO THE *PIECE CORPS* IN COLOMBIA A CERTAIN LUST FOR LIFE THAT MANIFESTED ITSELF IN UNORTHODOX WAYS.

Carl having a turn at bull fighting in Colombia in 1967 when he was in the Peace Corps. It was "lots of fun" but he was hit in the back by a bull and had to have extensive back and shoulder surgery.

In Cali, Colombia, in 1965 during the summer clinic at Universidad del Valle. Carl at far left. Pedro Gonzales (second from the right) went to the Olympic Games in 1968 in Mexico City and took fourth place in the 200 meter event.

Street kids in Peace Corps days outside the National Stadium in Cali, Colombia.

Lifters in Colombia during the Peace Corps period. All were
South American champions.

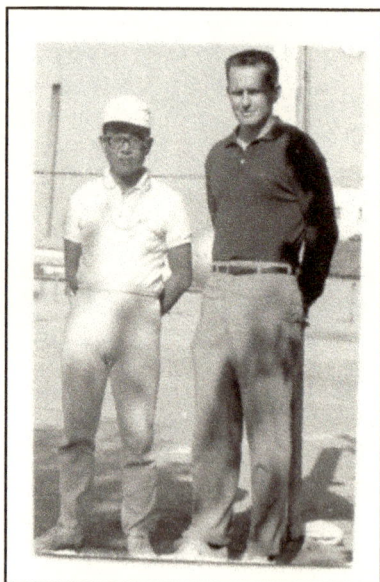

Carl with Yashi Tanaka, Japanese
National Coach, in 1967.

Carl in 1967 with Japanese lifters and coach Hari Haraikawas.

Sandra with parents in 1967. She grew up in Sault Sainte Marie,
Michigan and Long Beach, California.

Bob Hoffman outside York Barbell plant, York, Pennsylvania, circa 1975. He is considered to be the father of American weightlifting.

Clarence Bass and Carl competed in the National
Teenage Championships in 1957. He is near
eighty in this photograph taken in 2002. He is
from Albuquerque, New Mexico and a physical
fitness councilor at the time of this book's
publication.

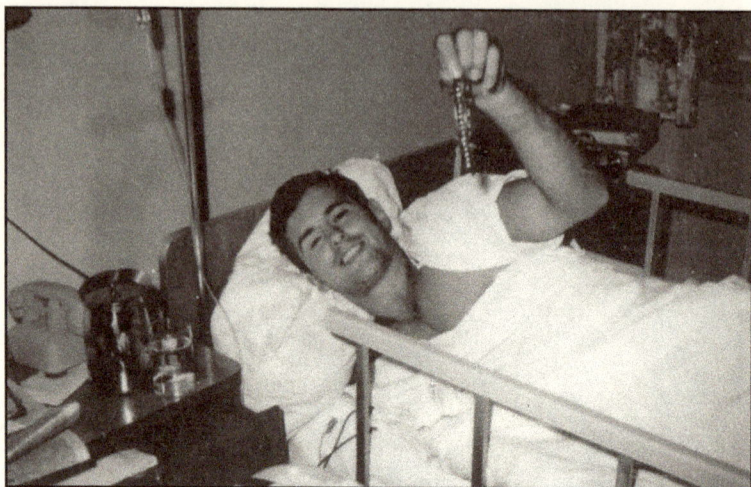

Carl in Chicago in 1968 after his second back surgery holding a device that had been implanted in his back in Japan and removed by Dr. Jimmy Stack.

Tommy Kono, probably in 1952. He was voted the best American lifter ever, having won in two Olympic Games, six National Championships and was Mr. Universe in 1954 and 1958.

Carl's stepfather, Lenard Kenith McRae, and Sandra. McRae was the reason Carl began weightlifting in 1952 when McRae took him to Bert Goodrich's gym on Hollywood Boulevard. Carl was almost thirteen at the time.

Mike Karchut, National and World Lifting Champion. His lifting career spanned the 1970s and early 1980s. He was always helping other lifters and lives in Billings, Montana at the time of this book's publication.

Mark Cameron was a top world competitor from Rhode Island. He was coached by Joe Mills in the 1970s and 1980s. He placed fourth several times in World Championships and Olympics.

Genaldi Ivanchenko was an Olympic champion in 1972 and 1976 representing the USSR. He was known for his muscular back.

Kyle in fifth grade lifting sixty pounds with excellent style. His best lift was 205 pounds overhead.

Carl with sons Shane (left), and Kyle.
Both excelled at lifting, school and many sports.

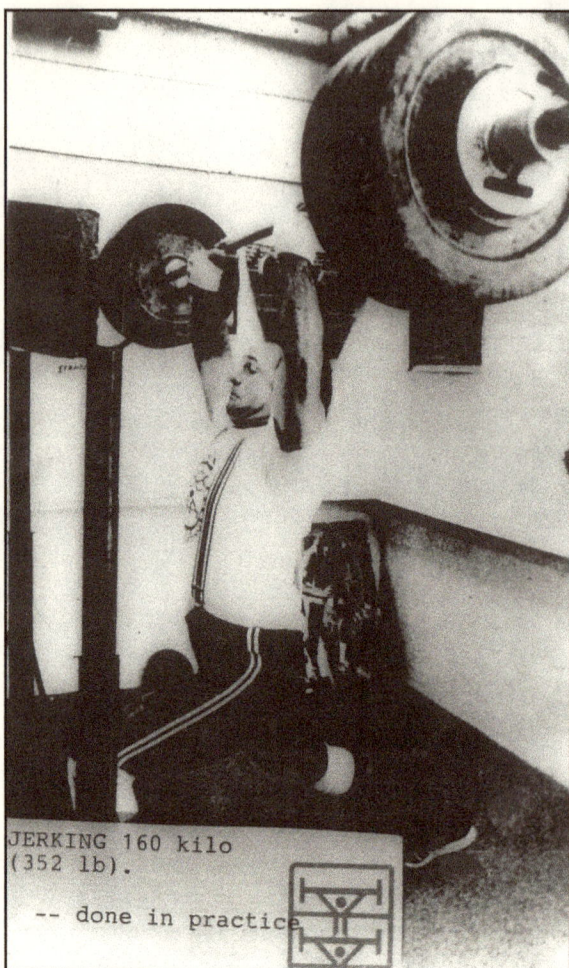

JERKING 160 kilo
(352 lb).

-- done in practice

Carl in 2003 jerking 352 pounds at Carlos Gilbert
Elementary School in Santa Fe, New Mexico. He
always lifted to keep in shape and still does at
age 78 when this book was published.

Carl, "dressed to the nines" in 2006 lifting 248 pounds for a magazine photograph. Note the vest and the humor of it all.

Carl and a show of abs in 2002 for a magazine feature, notable even in this fuzzy photograph.

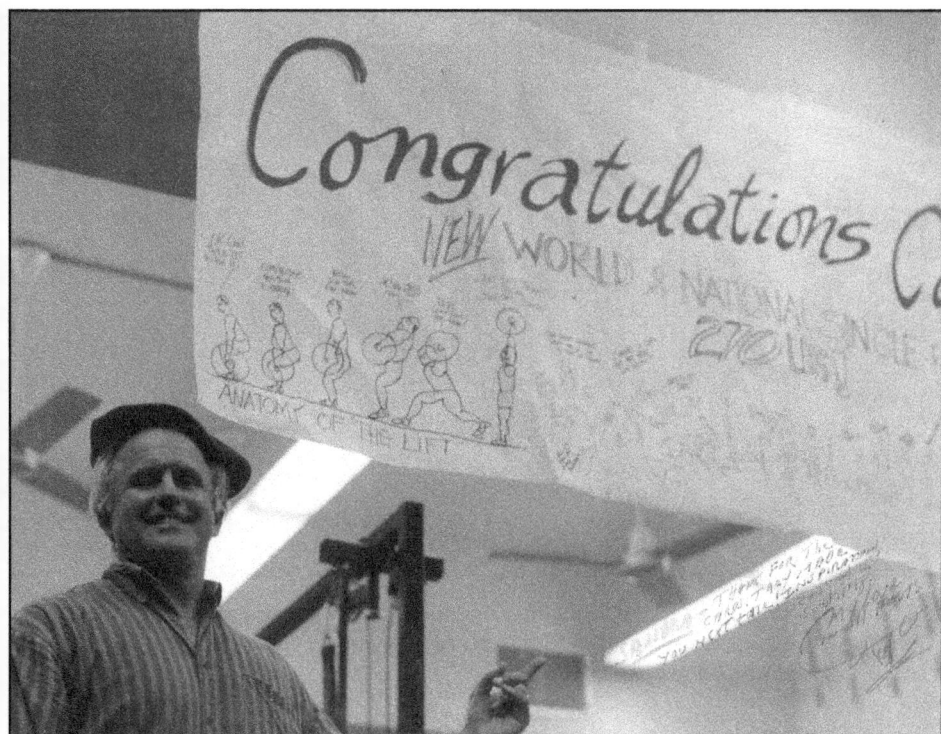

Carl when he got back from a regional competition in 1998 enjoying the sign at their gym put up by gym members.

Carl on the Santa Fe City Council. He was elected in 1980 and served full term until 1984. He spearheaded the founding of a Community Foundation, and the expansion of Valdez Industrial Park.

John Stephenson came into Carl and Sandra's gym for shoulder rehab and got involved in Olympic Style Lifting. This photograph was taken in 1997. He lifted until he was 98 years old.

Kyle in 2002 when he was a National Chess Champion.

4

Japan

My Invitation To Japan

As I mentioned earlier, the officials for the Japanese women's volleyball team had seen the progress made by the athletes and others when we were in South America and in the summer of 1964 they asked me if I would come to Japan and weight train their volleyball team. They wanted to jump higher and cover the court faster. I had agreed but I told them I needed other jobs to make enough to live on. So they contacted the Hankyu Braves, a Japanese baseball team and I was hired by that team to increase their speed, batting and throwing power. And I also got a job doing exercise physiology research at Mikage University as well as a job setting up a physical education program at an international school. So I had a full schedule for the almost all of the three years I was in Japan.

While there I learned a lot about warming up, nutrition, flexibility training, and variations in lifting styles. The Japanese were very friendly toward me—probably influenced by their memories of Coach Bob Hoffman who had trained one of their lifters at his training center in York, Pennsylvania.

When Lynn and I decided and agreed to go to Japan, my dad was furious. He had fought many brutal battles in the Pacific against the Japanese.

Boat To Japan

We traveled to Japan on a ship with many Japanese passengers. At night we were shown movies but many of them were American movies showing battles between Americans and Japanese. After seeing these movies night after night I felt uneasy since almost all the passengers were Japanese and these American movies showed America always winning. I got to know two Japanese fairly well and I asked them what they thought about the movies. They said, "Action good but American forces always winning and Japanese losing! What a lousy PR man who had charge of these movies!"

The Japanese passengers got back at me by playing against me in water polo in the ship's pool. But I managed to even the score by taking them all on in boxing—I had fought golden gloves in Southern California and fought two years on the University of California boxing team, as I've already mentioned.

We landed in Yokohama, a port city south of Tokyo.

Train To Kobe Station

From Yokohama we took a train that that could reach a 100 miles per hour plus. Just as we were leaving we felt a sudden impact. Later I asked one of the Japanese passengers if he knew what had happened and he said a student had committed suicide. He said it was an honorable way of doing it. The same as committing Hara-Kari with a knife. Since Japan was famous for its fast trains, this fell into the category of an honorable way of doing it.

But on a lighter note, the ride on the bullet train was breathtaking. Imagine going over 100 miles an hour between two cites: Tokyo to Kobe—a very, very fast trip. So before long we were at Kobe train station. Kobe had been rebuilt almost entirely since it had been destroyed during WWII.

Kobe

It turned out that my main job was to implement a full scale physical education and athletic program at an international school for grades one through twelve. And it was a good place with excellent public transportation. The building facilities had just been completed. It had a full size basketball court and gymnastic facility that would make any college facility envious. All the teachers and the headmaster were supportive.

Women's Volleyball

I also had two programs to build on. One was in Osaka where the Nichibo factory, a textile manufacturer, sponsored the Nichibo Volleyball Team. They employed the tallest women they could find to work there and would have them train for international athletic competitions. The women worked in various departments from maintenance to managerial. They worked from eight in the morning until four in the afternoon and then from four-thirty to ten-thirty that night they practiced volleyball every day. I'd never seen such long, grueling practice anywhere. I got to work with them from nine to ten-thirty in the evening twice a week. I was to make them jump higher and cover the court faster. They managed to do this and went to the Olympics in 1968 where they won first. I asked two of the women how they could train so hard and for such a long time. They told me they'd do anything for their country.

Pro Baseball

The other big job I had was to work with one of their professional baseball teams. Baseball is very popular in Japan.

Research At Mikage University

I was also involved with research in exercise physiology at Mikage University. It was there that training at high altitude produced more endurance was demonstrated, but it had the bad side effect of an athlete getting too hot. That is because red blood cells have a great capacity for storing up heat. This was shown in the 1984 Olympic held in Los Angeles. From 5000 meters on up, athletes who had trained at altitude felt the Los Angeles heat and their performances showed it.

The Denver Broncos were also aware of this. They were partially able to remedy this by going to the Super Bowl two weeks before and getting acclimated.

Jobs For Retired Athletes

In Japan I was impressed with how they took care of their athletes. After their participation and winning in the Olympics, they had jobs prepared for them. I was very interested in how they adapted to their jobs and I found out that they did very well. I asked this because after such hard dedication for years I wanted to know how life treated them after that. Later on when I did some work for the San Francisco 49ers I found out that they had a person in charge of steering their players into appropriate jobs as well. When you think of being a top football player starting at grade school level and all the adulation one had for so many years and that is all that you have done, there could be a big let down. This can be true in any sport where you were number one all the time.

My Observations Of The Japanese People

While I was in Japan I noticed how much the people seemed to appreciate spring flowers. Spring was celebrated with all kinds of flowers, especially cherry blossoms and daffodils. An older individual on our street once told me that he just lived to see another spring.

Winter was cold and humid but then spring came and summer was hot and humid. Humidity was common to all seasons. Transportation was by bus and rail, both very efficient. About ninety percent of the population lived on about ten percent of the land. Most of Japan is mountainous and used for cattle ranching, skiing, and climbing.

The legal system is used sparingly. People seemed to work out their differences face to face. For example, a neighbor had a young child drown in their pool. In the USA they might go to court and sue. At the time I was told only about ten percent of the problems would go to court, even this one tragedy, which, if can believe it, was settled by the two parties out of court. I was told that Japan had one-tenth of the lawyers as the USA. There is a lot of peer pressure not to go to court.

There is also a great sense of cooperation between the people. I was told that after WWII sports became a way to learn this. As we all know it takes great cooperation to succeed at a high level in sports.

The Japanese also seemed to compartmentalize their lives. When you worked, you worked. Period. When you had fun, you had fun. Period. I found that when they were to play or drink they would laugh a lot. When they were at work, not so much. There was not so much overlapping as there is in other cultures. Everything and everybody in its place. For example, if you did a job you did it to the best of your ability as an individual and as a team. So each one takes their place seriously in order to earn respect for one's self as well as the respect of their co-workers and place in society.

Two of the big sport teams I worked with, the Nichibo Volleyball Team and Hankyu Braves baseball team were good examples of these traits.

As I mentioned, baseball is a very popular sport in Japan. Some Japanese played in major league in the USA. And some major league players in the US came over to play in Japan. They had signed into their contract that they were not going to practice like the Japanese! Too hard and unnecessarily so.

I observed that the Japanese were very hard working and meticulous people. They are very family oriented and the individuals I worked with got up early. Many of them would exercise before they went to work or even when they were at work. In good weather they would exercise on the roofs during their breaks at work.

In the cold months, the heat in Japanese houses involved taking a one and a half foot heater from room to room. Another way was to soak in a hot wooden tubs.

In my experiences not many of them discussed the atom bombs dropped on Hiroshima and Nagasaki. Some of the older Japanese told me that they thought the Americans were going to slaughter them and were surprised when they didn't. I heard from some Japanese that the

Americans won because our god was greater than their god. When I think about WWII and the brutality of it, it's hard to believe that we are such allies today.

I was told that there was a general feeling of gratitude that the USA allowed them to keep their emperor and protect them from the Soviets and Chinese.

Side Trips to Other Countries

While in Japan, I had the opportunity to travel to Communist China, South Korea, Taiwan and India. As a result of these experiences, I have given many talks on the various cultures of these countries.

China

I had the chance to go to China because the Japanese were going on an invitation as one of the emerging nations. Americans were not allowed in China, so the Japanese did a great makeover to make me look oriental. I didn't think it was very convincing but I went along with it.

The plane we took had its windows blacked out as were all the window of the train we took later and the car that picked us up. When we were dropped off at a dormitory we noticed that the windows were also covered. We had constant guards in and around our doors. The windows of our bus were also covered when we were transported from the dormitory to the training and competition building. They even covered all the windows of the training and competing building.

When we arrived in Beijing we were given comfortable sleeping and eating accommodations but we were not to take anything "Beijing" out of China.

I found the weightlifting organization, athletes, officials, coaches and trainers to be very friendly and helpful. They treated us very well. Years later, in 1978, when the World Weightlifting Championships were held in Gettysburg, Pennsylvania I remembered some of the lifters who were now coaches and trainers. And everyone on the Chinese team remembered me. It was a nice meeting.

South Korea

A few years later there was an International Conference in Seoul, Korea. The South Koreans were very friendly to us. They were grateful for the Americans who fought to save their country in WWII. There were many atrocities that were still fresh in the Koreans' memories so there were bad feelings between the Koreans and the Japanese.

India

In 1968 while I was in Japan the Japanese Weightlifting Association sent me to Allahabad, India to teach track and field, volleyball, and weightlifting. We flew to Calcutta and then took a train to Allahabad which is located on the Ganges River. The family we stayed with was quite religious and highly respected in their community. The grandfather was writing his memoirs. He had spent years in a British jail and the experience had increased his faith. His son, in whose house we were staying, was on one of the High Courts of India. He was very active and introduced us to his teammates on the national cricket team. Sometimes this game could go for six hours.

Our stay in Allahabad was during the Christmas season. Although the majority of the people were not Christians, Christmas is one of the holidays that is celebrated. We were invited to several parties and one of the guests at one party was the future prime minister, Indira Gandhi. A question put to her during one of our conversations was, "What is democracy?" She replied, "A river with banks."

During our free time we took sightseeing trips by bus, train, car, elephant, riverboat, bike, and even on foot. India is huge and has many languages and customs, There are many different ways of living, yet the people I encountered seemed to get along well with each other. While India has a history of political unrest, none of it impacted on my stay there and I enjoyed my experience.

Tommy Kono

Coming back we stopped for a few days in Hawaii and looked up

Tommy Kono. He was considered pound for pound the best lifter in the world. When asked about this he said the international medals were always won against the lifters from other countries that were the best, and this brought out the best in him. He set a world record as a middle heavyweight (weight limit 90 kg (198 pounds)). In the course of winning these championships, Kono set 37 American, 8 Pan American, 7 Olympic, and 26 world records. He is the only weightlifter to set world records in four separate weight divisions. Though known chiefly as a weightlifter, Kono also won physique (bodybuilding) titles: Mr. World in 1954 and Mr. Universe in 1955, 1957, and 1961. And Tommy was always humble. Quite a man.

Boxer Joe Brown and Corner Man Billy Defoe

In 1967 in Columbia, Billy DeFoe a corner man and cut man for pro boxers took former world lightweight champ Joe Brown to fight in Cali. I was stunned to see what a corner man can do. Joe had a severe cut under his right eye and Billy had that closed in seconds and did the same with a big welt cheek that was ready to burst. And it was interesting to see what Joe Brown did with all that money from his boxing match—all clothes and especially shoes. He had more shoes than Imelda Marcos, the former first lady of Ferdinand Marcos, dictator of the Philippines.

A few days after the match Billy wanted to learn to fish with a net. It was really a sight to see this short man with a cigar in his mouth, wading, and then falling down in the stream trying to net some fish. When he left Billy said we would keep in touch always. And we did until Billy died ten years later.

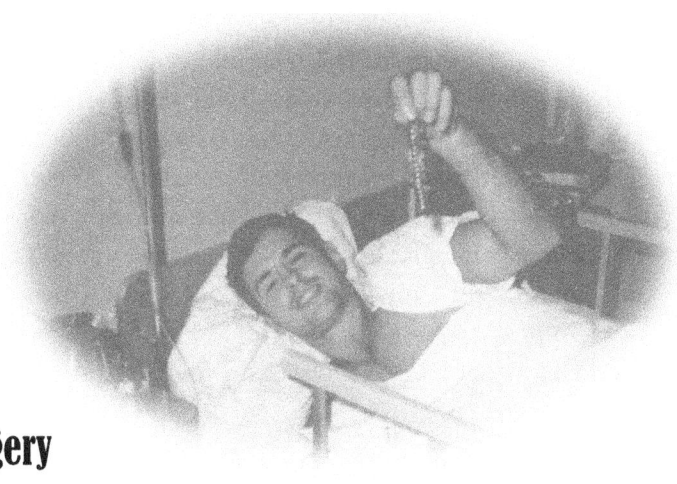

5

Back Surgery

Japan

In 1968, my last year in Japan, I had my back operated on as the pain from the bull incident in Colombia had gotten worse. The surgeons put me under and chipped away damaged bone in the lower five vertebrae and then stabilized the area with rods—something like an erector set. I was in the hospital for three months during which time I couldn't even sit up. I was told not to do hard exercise for a year—only walk. But at the end of a year the pain was still there. The Japanese surgeons finally told me that the operation just did not work.

Chicago

I couldn't go on with this kind of pain which was getting worse so leaving Japan I flew to Chicago to see Dr. Jimmy Stack. I had to check in with my dad anyway so the timing was perfect. (See details earlier in this book.) Dr. Stack fixed my shoulder and then also removed the metal erector set and performed state-of-the-art repair on the five vertebra. He told me he was surprised that the Japanese operated the way they did, that this kind of operation hadn't been done in forty years. It was the same type of operation that President Kennedy had and that hadn't worked either.

I was in bed only six days and released from the hospital after one month. I felt good. The back didn't hurt and the shoulder was fine. Within six months I could do anything. My lower back had fused well and my shoulders were tight. No pain, no loss of movement with the exception of certain back movements. I couldn't do gymnastic flips, but the shoulder was well enough that I could swing on the rings. The operation had been a great success. All these years later and I haven't experienced any pain and the only sport activities I haven't been able to do are golf and gymnastics. As soon as I healed up I started lifting heavy weights and in 1974 set a USA record Masters of 281 snatch and 352 clean and jerk weighing 197.

6

Santa Fe, New Mexico

In 1968, after our stint in Japan and my successful back operation, my wife Lynn and I settled in Santa Fe, New Mexico, where Lynn was born. Santa Fe is a small city which is the oldest capital in the United States, 7,000 feet above sea level, with four mild seasons. One can ski, hike, go river rafting, and fish. It is considered an art center and has many music organizations. New Mexico is a tri-cultural state—Anglo, Hispanic and Native American. So we all learn from each other.

Because Santa Fe at its lowest altitude is 6,800 to 10,000 at highest altitude, we get a variety of athletes who come to train at altitude. We once had a research team of track and field athletes and coaches. One famous study done in Santa Fe was to see the effects of altitude training on endurance sports and another was on the effects of heat and cold on athletes. Santa Fe was the first place where studies on heat and cold were performed. Heat and cold effects first came to the attention of the sports world during the Olympics in Los Angeles in 1984. It was hot there and times were way slower than usual. That brought lots of interest in determining the effect different degrees of heat did what. As for altitude, it would seem that for every 500 feet there is a significant increase in strength gain.

Fred Martiniz, Sense of Humor

And just an aside, but an important one, a sense of humor I have learned through the years is very productive. I want to give an example. Fred Martinez of Santa Fe used comedy to earn money to go to college. He developed into a real comedian. And he was so quiet! He proposed to his wife on a comedy club stage! He told me you bring people along, and then make a joke or a funny statement. He has done this many times with me. As I said he is very quiet, an engineer, and also a national caliber Olympic weightlifter.

Santa Fe Preparatory School and Scouting with Vernon Samorian

Meanwhile, my first job, as I mentioned earlier, when I first moved to Santa Fe was at Santa Fe Preparatory School teaching Russian history and coaching the soccer and basketball teams, weightlifting, and track and field. I taught and coached there for two years. I raised money for our trips to competitions by going out into the community and asking for donations, just as I did as a college weightlifter. I used the "Green Hornet" to drive members of my teams to competitions.

Some of our trips took us to such places as Denver, Tulsa, Berkeley, El Paso, Tucson and Phoenix. We did well on these trips and the Prep lifters set national teenage records. They had a great lifting style and made very good impressions. It was their performances as well as my later successes with foreign teams that gave me the visibility that resulted in my later becoming the National Weightlifting Coaching Coordinator for the Olympics.

During that time I also did a lot of basketball scouting for Prep. Our first trip was to Penasco, a small town northeast of Santa Fe in the mountains. I took assistant coach Vernon Samorian, originally from Massachusetts, with me. After we observed the game we went to a local pub to go over what we had seen. It was a nice place and Vernon looked around and noticed that some of the people were paying for their beers and drinks with food stamps. This infuriated Vernon. This didn't go over well at all with Vernon, a hot Greek from a part of the country where such behavior was really frowned on. He yelled and screamed and pretty soon there was a fight.

I told Vernon to shut up but no such luck. There were over fifty people in this small pub so I ended up crawling on the floor to get out. I couldn't see where Vernon was but I heard him calling the people thieves and robbers and worse. Well, I crawled out in about half an hour but Vernon was going at it with fists, legs, chairs, and bottles. He was quite a mess when he finally got out. He asked, "What happened to you? Where were you?" I told him I wanted to stay in one piece so I crawled out. He thought that was funny. I didn't care what he thought. I was safe.

And believe it or now, the very next Saturday night at a lounge in downtown Santa Fe, we went in to go over the basketball game we had just seen. It was really crowded and suddenly a fight broke out and two people got knifed in the stomach. I guess I soon learned my lesson about discussing basketball games in bars and lounges.

While at Prep I would often go to weightlifting clinics. I usually took two or three lifters from Prep to help me. One was Timmy Ortiz, national teenage champion at the age of 15 and then again at age 16 and 17. Timmy's concentration was amazing. He could be talking one minute to somebody and in the next moment instantly respond to, "Timmy, you are up to lift." He was exact on his lifts and was fun to work with because of his attitude. He always said, "It's fun to lift." Many, many lifters don't hold that attitude and become overly serious in their concentration.

We once went to Cuba, New Mexico where they had a lifting team under the direction of Juan Garcia who also had a Dairy Queen in Santa Fe. One of their lifters, Jose Delgado, really enjoyed the activity. It seems that some places just bring out the best attitude and performance. Later, in the five times we went there, Delgado made state records every time.

During 1966 I also joined up with an organization called Athletes in Action and worked with a group of inmates in the state penitentiary outside Santa Fe. A good friend of the family was in there for multiple car thefts. He would tell me about each prisoner as they lifted. Most of the time, he said that each prisoner had a sob story as to why he was in the pen. But many of them turned their lives around and came out of prison totally rehabilitated. One such individual thought lifting Olympic-style helped his rehabilitation because it gave him confidence that he could improve in other areas. But it was argued in some circles that Olympic-style lifting made prisoners so strong they could beat up on fellow prisoners.

At least in the prisons I went to this never happened and it didn't happen when they were released. I had gone to four prisons—San Quintin, California; Stafford, Arizona; Santa Fe, New Mexico; and Baltimore, Maryland. Some of the lifters got so good they tried out for the Olympic team. One made it and you can imagine the logistics of taking prisoners out of prison to compete and then returning them. But we worked it out. He lifted in the Rome Olympics and placed in the top ten. He was guarded the entire time and we safely returned him.

Running For Political Office

Living in one place and settled down after traveling so much had many advantages. Santa Fe, as I said earlier is a mixture of three cultures, Anglo, Hispanic and Native American. When I came back to New Mexico and Santa Fe for good after being in Colombia for two years, Japan for three and all the travel I did in the Far East and South America, I was very much interested in politics and what the Republican Party stood for at that time. In 1968 a St. John's graduate, Don Stillwell, and I went around in an old Ford truck campaigning for Nixon. Now this was in northern New Mexico and Republicans were outnumbered by 4-1, yet going door to door, mile after mile, we did very well. And we got to know a lot of people and learned about their culture and political interests and leanings and they got our beliefs on many things including politics and culture.

My dad thought we were nuts, going into a mainly Spanish areas and outnumbered by those odds. But we made a difference and he admitted it when I told him some of our experiences. Then two years later, I ran for the State Legislator. The district I would represent had the same 4-1 odds. I was still teaching at the time at Santa Fe Prep. They initially said I could run and retain my position teaching history and physical education. Then in the mid-summer the first poles came out and I was trailing my opponent by only four points in nearby areas Tesuque and Pojoaque. Santa Fe Prep was a very liberal and democratic-leaning school. With these poles being what they were I was told that I would have to choose between teaching at Prep and running for office. But I really wanted to campaign and my dad said go ahead and he would support me. It turned out he didn't so I quit teaching and coaching anyway and finished the campaign, which I lost. So here I was losing the race, no money and my wife six months pregnant with our second child.

Working at Empire Builders

So with a failed campaign behind me and during Santa Fe Fiesta time, I ran into Henry Culver who owned Empire Builders. I had met Henry while teaching at Santa Fe Prep. He sponsored our weightlifting team and had been impressed that our lifters were so talented and had won five national teen-age championships. Henry really appreciated the way I had taught and coached his son and daughter at Prep and he offered me a job at about twice what I had been making at the Prep. Hell, I didn't know a brick from a block, but my job from Monday to Friday was selling blocks and bricks to architects and builders. On Saturdays, I was in the store selling hardware equipment. I didn't know anything about that either but Henry encouraged me to be patient, assuring me that I would learn.

Well, I was making good money but didn't much like the job. Everything was great, Henry co- workers, clients. And it even offered me the opportunity to travel and make and renew contacts with Republican leaders in the state. But after two years I almost had a nervous break-down. I just did not the like the work and I was not learning well. I told Henry my problem. I really wanted to learn and please him and others in the business. Henry tried to take the pressure off me by saying that I was doing well and would adjust. My dad thought I was crazy to feel that way about a good job, as did many friends.

I decided that I needed to get away and think. So my wife and two sons took a trip out to California to visit friends and relatives. I knew I did not want to teach at junior high, senior high or college level but one day I took the time to visit my nephew in elementary school. Suddenly it dawned on me that I wanted to teach and coach at the elementary level, as it seemed to be a very meaningful time for these young students. So when we came back I took courses to earn my elementary teaching certificate. During this time I supported my family by working at a gas station. It was fun.

Teaching Elementary School

In the summer of 1972 after getting my certificate there were no jobs available so I ran recreational programs for the City of Santa Fe at Carlos Gilbert Elementary school. I called up Eddie Ortiz, Superintendent of Elementary Education to inquire about jobs and he told me not to worry that a job will open up where you are. I thanked him but expressed concern about two teachers there running summer programs I thought were not up to their jobs. He told me that those two teachers would be transferred to another school. I thought that was strange, but it happened—one of them was even made principal of another elementary school! I thought that was even more strange, getting rid of a bad teacher by making him principal of another elementary school, but it worked out well for me. A week before school started I was given the job of teaching fifth and sixth grade history and science and eventually became vice principal. I was there for ten years and did an excellent job, if I do say so myself, and was liked by the principal, teachers and students and I felt a great deal of accomplishment.

Because of my successful teaching, the parents and teachers wanted me to start an elementary physical education program. The principal, parents and teachers voted unanimously to take two more students per classroom, freeing me to develop and start a full physical education program for grades one to six. We had intramurals for team sports two days a week and intramurals for individual sports two days a week. Many times we received awards for the best physical education program of all the schools in state and we didn't even know we were being judged.

My future wife Sandra who was a part time teacher at the school helped me with intramural and after school programs. She was and is a born teacher of anything. The sports I taught were football, basketball, baseball, gymnastics, boxing, ultimate Frisbee and the new Olympic sport—team handball. We were the only school to do this. And this because the principal and teachers wanted it, Olympic-style weightlifting and wrestling.

We had ten years of greatness before the principal, Elvin McCalister, retired and the physical education and enrichment programs were dropped by the new principal. This move was challenged by parents and teachers who took their case to the Board of Education to lobby for reinstatement but to no avail.

My opinion at that time was that there was a culture of mediocrity in the school system. It appeared to me that the school system awarded salary increases based on the number of years an individual had been teaching, not by how well the teachers were doing and how well the students were doing.

There were many excellent programs under the leadership of Elvin McCalister. And he always stood up for his teachers. After he retired I stayed two more years. But with our physical education program and other enrichment programs dismantled I began to think about another line of work. It was then I asked myself what other skills I had and it turned out that I really knew the gym business. So I left the school system and got together with two physical therapists I knew who had the same interests and we opened up a combined gym/physical therapy business at what was then the Girl Scout building.

As a point of interest, I used to ride my mini bike from home to our gym. It would take about twenty minutes. It was a great bike, but one time the front frame collapsed and the handles went right into my thighs. Lots of pain and blood. I was close to the gym so I got gauze and tape and stopped the bleeding and went on with my day. I will talk more about the gym business later.

National Weightlifting Coaching Coordinator

I spoke earlier of Bob Hoffman and the York Barbell Company. Bob and his company organized, started and nursed along Olympic-style lifting in the United States. His teams were national and world champions. My coach back when I was younger, as I've mentioned, Frank Spellman, was on one of those teams when he worked for York Barbell. Like others on the York team he became an Olympic champion. In the 1960s Bob got disenchanted with Olympic weightlifters. To him he had done everything for them and they did little in return. So his interest turned to other sports and American lifting went downhill. To many, the sport was dying.

Then along came Bob Chris, National Director of the National Weightlifting Committee. Through his efforts and leadership Bob decided that we needed a national program. And he picked up very capable support from the National Weightlifting Committee. Clarence Bass of Albuquerque, New Mexico also agreed. He was a player, published physical training books, and was a top Olympic lifter. They and the rest of the committee knew many talented, hardworking people and they all came aboard. But Bob Crist was the one who had made it all come together. In 1972 they advertised for a National Weightlifting Coaching Coordinator.

The National Weightlifting Committee and representatives from other Olympic sports had a meeting at the Muehlebach Hotel in Kansas City (where Harry Truman gave his acceptance speech). Candidates for the job were interviewed one at a time to present a plan. Members of the committee were very well known to the public. Jack Kelly, Olympic Gold medalist and brother to Princess Grace Kelly, was such a member.

Back during the same time that I was teaching at the Elementary School, I had started a small weightlifting team in the school and our sponsors raised enough money so we could do some traveling. Our lifters received a lot of attention. We had many national teenage champions and record holders. The success we had reached the level that when the National Weightlifting Committee wanted a national teen-age camp I was chosen as the coach. After a few years coaching these camps, I had built up a good reputation and this led up to my being asked to apply for the position of national Olympic weightlifting coach.

The plan I submitted was to travel the country setting up weightlifting clubs and recruiting coaches and athletes in Olympic-style weightlifting. Well I was chosen, but they wanted me to move to Indianapolis, Indiana and have that as my base of operation. I explained that I couldn't accept under that condition. And that was that for the time being.

I had always wanted to become a national Olympic weightlifting coach. There wasn't a national coach in any sport. But that was to change. At the 1972 Olympic Games in Munich our athletes didn't do well—especially the big name sports of track and field, basketball and swimming. The Iron Curtain teams had national teams and they had many successes in international competition. The USA executives because of our poor showing in Munich decided it was going to have such a program in one sport and see what happened. Well, they were not going to start such a program in a highly visible sport so they chose weightlifting, not a highly visible sport in the USA at the time. In years past, the USA had great teams, but as the Iron Curtain countries nationalized their teams we fell way back. This started back in the 1950s.

As I said, all my life I wanted that coaching position. And it did not even exist until 1972 when I had originally presented my plan. Turning that position down was a real hard decision that tore me apart. But I had to do it. I thought I would never get another chance. But a year later they called me and said they wanted me and my plan without restrictions on my home base. I accepted and got to work and by 1976 the USA had won four silver medals.

In spite of this success and other factors, Bob Crist resigned as National Director and so did many members of the committee. I hung around until 1978 and then got disgusted and also resigned. Internal problems arose in the committee and it became apparent that the committee was not going to change and would not for some time.

So after I resigned I ran for and won a seat on the Santa Fe City Council and was elected to the Santa Fe Water Board, and also opened up our gym that was successful for decades. More on this later.

Building the National Program and Developing Champions

At the time, I was still vice principal at Carlos Gilbert and taught Monday through Friday mornings. My duties included finding established good lifters, train coaches and find facilities to train at. We called them clinics. The administration at the elementary school let me travel Thursday to Sunday for the Olympic lifting program and the Olympic and World Championships. I went to small towns like Hays, Kansas and Safford, Arizona as well as to big cities like New York, Atlanta, Dallas, Chicago, Seattle, St. Louis, Denver, Napolian, Cleveland, Bozeman, and Green Bay, Wisconsin. We wanted assurance that the individuals I would meet had the tremendous desire to be the best they could be. When we had this kind of individual we supported the individual. And this took a lot of skill and the will to win. We spent much time setting the groundwork so the clinics well attended.

In that program we counseled the fifth and sixth grade on what activities they would probably do well in as they got older. I based this on several measurements including leverages of their limbs to each other and their body lengths to each other. Body leverages were the most important. For example, if an upper leg was smaller in proportion to the whole leg, one would have better leverage. If an upper arm was less in proportion than the whole arm, then one would have better upper arm leverage. And so it went.

I found that leverage was more important than muscle mass or muscle quality. Maybe you have wondered how one person can generate more speed and power than another. All things being equal, it is because one person has better leverage than another. Just that simple.

In scouting around the US, some things really stood out. We found that the top prospects came from the wrestling and gymnastics athletes. And some lifters really wanted to win and others not so much in spite of all the talent they had. They felt too much pressure if they won and they didn't want that. This really surprised me but was a reality I had never considered. I thought that everybody who was competent would want to make the Olympics. Not so.

An important element is how the athletes live their lives. Good sleeping and eating habits, no drinking of liquor or smoking no carousing at night. It came as a surprise to me that this wasn't the case with some very, very talented individuals. Why some of the most talented lifters did not clean up their acts was a mystery to me. I mean most of these lifters had trained very, very hard and not to take care of themselves was beyond comprehension. And it cost them their chance to be on the Olympics team. And it cost the whole program if the top lifters weren't pushed as hard as they should have been. This is something very important in an individual sport. The members who are competing to make the Olympic team should push each other.

It was during this time that I began to realize that many lifters do not achieve their goals because to reach them a lifter must be what I call a real connoisseur. You have to know why you want to do it. If they don't know that, they don't know how to get there. Then they have to work hard, and they have to eliminate errors and omissions. They must not be afraid of getting to the top because once you get there, there is less competition. They have eliminated themselves and have found their niche.

In about two years we knew which athletes were promising and we concentrated on the individuals in those last two years before the Olympic tryout. We also knew which coaches and administrators would be the best and we encouraged them to continue. At this point we had fewer coaches and administrators, and we gave them more attention. I then cut back on scouting because we felt that we had identified the best.

So we had our Olympic tryouts and took them through private training for two weeks before the Olympics. This paid off at the 1976 Olympics in Montreal as we won more medals than we had won in sixteen years. Two silvers and two bronzes.

After the games we elected a new board of directors. Even though they had seen the results they wanted to do things differently. We lobbied to use the system that had proven so successful with no success. I stayed on for two years and then resigned. I could see that the system the board wanted to pursue was not working and it was evident that they were not going to change.

A Word About Relaxation

On another subject, for the Pan American Championships back in 1974 in Mexico City I had a hypnotist make a tape recording on relaxation. So a week before the lifters were going to compete I told them what to expect on the tape. I told them that some would benefit enormously, some moderately so, and some not at all. In any case they were to remain quiet until the tape was over. The tape was twenty-five minutes long and it was imperative for them to remain quiet and be respectful. Some things on the tape would make some of them laugh.

One of the lifters was adamant that the tape was a waste of time. But the night before he was to lift he came to my door and asked for the tape. He could not sleep. He took the tape and player to his room. I did not discuss the tape with him until after his competition. He did very well, won three gold medals and bettered his marks by a lot. Later, when we were alone he said the tape allowed him to sleep and absorb the positive messages. So this was a success. The few thoughts expressed on the tape were absorbed and utilized. Any more was too much. Quality not quantity is what produces success.

Criticism and Goals

Another thing, and my dad had told me time and again, don't be afraid of criticism. Most everything you try to do will be criticized, whether you deserve it not. Just seems to be a bad side to human nature. As I have gone through my life I have found this to be true. Sometimes people will just not try to do something because they don't want to be criticized. As Teddy Roosevelt said, it is better to have been in the arena and lost than be amongst the timid who don't try. I think of this when I have seen outstanding, competitive athletes just quit trying. What a waste of talent and energy. And I have found it happens in any endeavor of life.

Maybe we should have some kind of training about quitting because of criticism for our kids and students and also our peers. Sometimes we don't even think about this because we are so close to certain situations. And when it comes to winning or losing, sometimes one wonders in the great every day just how much more effort do I have to give to become a winner, or avoid defeat. And if you do lose, what lessons did you learn in that great effort, or what did you actually win in losing. I have felt that this is very important. If you want to win then you must analyze the reason why or if you do not want to lose then you have got analyze that side of the issue. When doing this it is important to know that you are not going to learn all there is in one try, but you will learn.

I have talked to enough winners and losers to know that many people don't go over the game of winning or losing. Under high emotional stress many things about winning and losing can become apparent. This is a big aspect to bettering oneself or not. I know a person who is making a good living by being a critic in his field. And yes, they do build statues to critics! And I have known people who advance far or rapidly because they are just able to do it—to understand the results that can come from thinking about winning and losing in the right way.

Another one of the things I believe is important is to constantly set goals. It gives a continuing challenge to one's life and gives inspiration to those one comes in contact with. And recognize you only have so much energy, so use it wisely.

International Adventures and Observations

During my tenure as the National Weightlifting Coaching Coordinator I traveled to many places that gave me experiences on a local level that allowed me to know people on a personal basis. I went to the former USSR three times, and to Poland, Romania, England, France, Spain, and Bulgaria.

Communist Russia was tightly controlled. The first time I went to the USSR in 1974 I was trying to get rid of jet lag. A simple way for me to do this is to jog. In spite of seeing Red Square many times in TV news reels, I didn't recognize it. Our hotel was right near there so I started out jogging and within five minutes, I was apprehended by three Soviet officers and taken to what seemed to be a holding area and interrogated. I was allowed to make one phone call so I called our the US Embassy. They began arranging for my release and warned me that Red Square was sacred because Lenin's tomb was there. So with a stern warning I was released after many hours. Wow, was I scared the whole time. Back at the hotel Bob Hise Sr., manager of the USA weightlifting team, read me the riot act!

One of the more enjoyable experiences I had in Moscow was being invited to meet Leonid Brezhnev. He asked me why we kicked out Nixon, that he was a great man and that he could always trust him and that they had built up a great trust between them. I thought at the time that this is a very difficult thing to do between leaders especially between two systems of government as different as the USSR and USA. When I left I felt I had a real insight into the personalities of Brezhnev and Nixon, that these were real people, not manikins. However, I was fully aware that Brezhnev kept a very tight hold on his people and that he could be ruthless.

On one of my trips to the USSR we had a competition in Tashkent which was Stalin's home town. The hotel we stayed in turned out to have some strange aspects. The lobby was modern, but as I was seated there one time I couldn't help but notice that every so often a person who seemed have been beaten up and in pain was brought up from a level below and taken outside to a car and taken away. This repeated itself several times during the days I was there. I asked several Russians what was happening. They simply said "dissidents" with a look that meant "say no more." I learned later that interrogations had been taking place below the lobby. So in this modern hotel we found out that there were almost medieval conditions and medieval tortures taking place.

At one of the world championships in the USSR, there were prostitutes trying to get in the hotel. They did this by phoning to the rooms the lifters were in. But the hotel security was very good and didn't let them in. In fact they didn't let anyone into the hotel unless they had a pass issued by the Moscow police or Russian KGB. One evening all the lifters in the competition were taken to a theater and were shown the contrast in living between the lives of Americans training and lifting and the Soviet training and lifting.

The American lifters were depicted as slovenly and the Soviet lifters as living a very strict and disciplined life. The film emphasized how the Soviets would win because they were disciplined and dedicated. The film was really hilarious because it was so extreme. Past Soviet champions then gave a propaganda talk. It was just too much.

The Worlds Championships where the Soviets won and the interviews with the winners were almost the same for each winner. The Soviet champions were asked, "How does it feel to win?" Almost all the Soviet winners said "Good, I won in the capital of the greatest country in the world." There was one exception. He made what I thought was the most unbelievable statement: "The heads of weightlifting are from the capital and they discriminate against other Russians. I am from Leningrad and so is my coach. They were not going to let my coach me, but then they changed their minds. If they hadn't, I wouldn't have lifted." I was shocked and I wondered what they were going to do with him. As far as I know, they did nothing. I believe it was because the Bulgarians had beaten the Russians two times previously and they needed this individual to lift and win. I mean, this was the World Championships being held in Moscow and to lose would have been such a downer. Bulgaria is about the size of Kansas and for big, mighty Russia to lose to them in the capital of their country would have been unthinkable.

It was here that I again met a former Soviet lifter we hadn't seen in years. I asked him where he had been and he said in he Gulag. What happened was there were four lifters who missed all their lifts and were beaten for the first time in years. One lifter had committed suicide, the other two escaped and he knew nothing more of them. He was the only lifter to get back into training and made this world championship team. He won these championships but only on his last attempt. He told a Soviet reporter that he was a Soviet citizen in the best country in the world and living in the greatest city in the world. He could not lose. Later in his room he told me his statement was pure propaganda. If he didn't win he would be sent back to the Gulag.

When we had free time we got students (for a price) to show us around. I asked about one Soviet premier in particular who was not entombed in the Kremlin wall. He told me that the premier had been banned but he would show me where he was buried. He took me out to a shabby cemetery where that disgraced former premier was buried. He showed me similar graves for individuals who had also fallen from favor.

The Bulgarians were a serious group. I showed a coach three post cards I had bought of Lenin. I said, "He must have been a popular man because he is on every card." He replied, "That is not funny. He was a great man and leader." I apologized but he didn't respond. I found out later that the Bulgarians of all the Soviet sphere lifters were very touchy when it came to Lenin. Bulgaria I was told felt strongly about Lenin and any discussion of the Soviets. Yet it was the Bulgarians who had beaten the USSR in the last two World Championships and the last Olympics in 1972.

Following one last competition in 1974 there was a big banquet with elegant food, and lots of it. I only mention this because all our meals up to that point were mainly cucumbers and mystery meat.

As we were leaving, we were closely watched all the way from our hotel to the airport and then frisked. Our plane landed at JFK and we were all glad to be on our way to our homes. I had bought some toys for my two boys. They were thrilled as they knew I had bought them in the Soviet Union.

Meanwhile, because of the political atmosphere, I had told our lifters not to expect too much from their friends or neighbors. And it turned out to be true for me as well. I had been home three weeks and all my neighbor said to me was that my dog had been into his garbage constantly. No greetings just that.

We were in Poland a couple of times. I found the Polish athletes and people to be very friendly. They would laugh and tell jokes on themselves. One was, "Did you hear about the Polish lifter who won a gold Medal? He had it bronzed!" And they liked to talk. They shared not only stories about weight lifting with me, but also about their personal lives. They shared many of their training secrets in lifting with us as well as their food. And they always wanted to know about the USA.I learned that Poland was considered a young country; for about 100 years Poland did not exist—it was part of another country. They had been invaded and occupied by Germany for a long time, and then by Communist Russia. It seemed to me that they were in many European conflicts and consequently occupied for years. When I was there they openly shared their experiences of being occupied during World War II. I found them to be very open, fun loving and smart—always looking to the future with hope and good expectations.

One time coming back from Poland we stayed a day in Latvia. Now part of the USSR, they were once an independent country and at one time a part of Germany. Part of the people have German ancestry and part Russian ancestry.

I had come into contact with some Polish people in Chicago, where I was born and partly grew up. There is a large Polish population in Chicago and in lifting they were many times the leaders in the number of championships won and world records gained. The USA weightlifting team had many Polish lifters who had performed very well over the years.

International Weightlifting Conference
in Bulgaria and Steroid Discussions

Later in the fall of 1974 I was sent to an international weightlifting conference in Sofia, Bulgaria. Boy, were we watched there. No matter where I went I always had "a trainer" with me. I was told that they didn't want me to get lost. The "trainers" were young college kids and were very friendly to me. I learned from them about the schools they went to, and their parents. They had very rigid academic programs and they were surprised that we were so kind and friendly. They had been told we were demons.

The Bulgarians always seemed guarded. Maybe this was because they had been abused by invading peoples in the past. While I was there, it seemed like a closed society, as if the Communists held tight control over them.

The Bulgarian long distance runners and lifters were among the best in the world. We kidded among ourselves that they were so good because of all the yogurt they ate! We actually thought they might have added a little something to it.

But our trips to Bulgaria were somewhat strange. On one hand I learned much about their training methods which included trips to the doctors. They came right out and said they used steroids but under doctors' supervision. That confirmed what we already suspected.

But steroids had already been used by the German athletes in the 1936 Olympic Games in Berlin. They had learned that steroids helped the athletes bulk up, have faster performance, and gain endurance. Records of this practice were found after the defeat of Nazi Germany in World War II.

We remember those Olympics because of the great performance of our Jesse Owens. But people forgot who won the team title—the Germans. We didn't then, but we now know how long they had been using steroids and the quantities. This opened up a big discussion during the conference on that and it became known that other top countries were also using them and in quantities, great quantities. The main part of the talk was that doctors felt these large doses were thought to be safe. So they really pushed the envelope on safety—at least many of us thought so at the time. There were a lot of opinions on this and one reason that steroids were considered safe is that no sickness or deaths had been reported. But, as I mention later, they are not safe.

What came out of these discussions was not whether lifters should use steroids—but how much was really safe. In view of this it was decided that no steroids should be used since no limits were known. It never came up on the morality of using steroids, just the safety issue. Many of us thought this was ridiculous. One lifter uses steroids, another so much more, and another nothing. What was moral or fair? So the conference came out with the statement that no steroids should be used and a strict test would be developed to test for them. Along with this came a cat and mouse game as athletes developed steroids that couldn't be detected, and then this was followed by the development of better tests.

Steroids were being used as far back as the 1880s in medical the field for patients who were badly burned or emaciated. These people had to put on muscle quickly to keep from dying. But then in time athletes used steroids to increase their performance. The results include gaining strength, muscle size and endurance. People usually don't know about the endurance part. I didn't, until I saw them used in middle and long distance events. Apparently, steroids act like an afterburner in mid and long distance.

One time, when I took the New Mexico Weightlifting Team to Tucson, Arizona to compete, there was a national shot champion who was obnoxious in the warm up room where lifters were warming up before they lifted in the competition. I learned later that he was a very avid user of steroids. Maybe that was one reason for his attitude.

In 1948 my coach Frank Spellman had already told me that the Soviets were surging to the top because of steroid use. He was offered steroids by the Soviets but didn't use them. By 1952 the Soviets were winning easily. That's when it became common, but they were banned, and testing for them was begun in earnest starting in the 1976 Olympic Games in Montreal, Canada. If athletes were caught, they were disciplined and the type of discipline depended on the sport. There have been athletes who have died because of steroid use.

The tests have gotten better and better and steroid use has gone down. But steroids have even been used by high school athletes. One of the big side-effects is very aggressive behavior and meanness. Many athletes have been known to use alcohol to come off the mood aggression and some have become alcoholics.

A chemical that was not discussed at our conference was HGH, human growth hormone. At that time and for some time after that it could not be detected. It wasn't in lifting that HGH came into vogue. But if you go through some of the track and field athletes' progress, it is evident that it had benefits, even more than steroids. Now it can be detected but it is a very expensive test and because of this it is not used all the time. It seems like in every endeavor, whether it is sports, business or government, there will always be cheaters. The vast majority of people are not cheaters and they should be protected from those who do.

The Bulgarians In Santa Fe

In the spring of 1978, two young men from Bulgaria came to Santa Fe and we had a great time. I took them to two different Indian Pueblos and to three feasts. We also went to a high school football game and this really interested them. They wanted to learn about baseball and of course they wanted to visit actual schools. I took them to Santa Fe High, as well as to a private school and also the University of New Mexico.

They really took to football. They said they wanted to play "boom, boom" and wanted to know how much they could earn playing at college level? Whey I told them, that sealed it. They were going to start football in their home towns and then back to the United States and try out for the pros. Money talks.

Visit From Japanese Secretary

On one occasion, a woman who had been my secretary when I had been in Japan came out to Santa Fe with her husband. She was very interested in our Native Americans. I took them to several pueblos along the Rio Grande and we arranged dates and times to meet. She and her husband who was from Canada really enjoyed learning about the Pueblo Indian way of life. She felt that they were similar to the Japanese because of their way of talking, eating, and relating to each other. As might be expected, she was very polite to the Indians and everybody she met. She felt especially attracted to the mountains, rivers and animals. And she felt the friendliness of the New Mexicans. We took her to weddings, parties, funerals, cultural events like the opera, political gatherings, school grades 1-2, the University of New Mexico, ranches, pueblos, military bases, and an air force base. As one knows, we don't have oceans, so we didn't do any "navy."

Clinics

Before we opened the gym and while I was still at Carlos Gilbert, we ran clinics for five years at what used to be the College of Santa Fe. The famed actress, Greer Garson, had the theatre-arts building named after her. She once made a real statement after her house burned down in Dallas. A reporter said, You lost all your pictures and movies. It must be devastating." She pointed to her head and said, "I have them all here."

I also ran training summer camps of four weeks each between 1978 and 2002 on other college campuses from Thursday to Sunday. Very successful. People thought they wouldn't sell well but they did. The camps required quite a bit of organization.

Selling the Clinics to Coaches

I had been looking over the Southwest: New Mexico, Arizona, Colorado, and West Texas for possible locations for our clinics. When I had something promising I would make an appointment with the coach and present a printed outline with photos of clinics I had conducted. I also included movies of the clinics. If I got a positive response from the coaches I would put together an agreement on how I would teach for those three or four days and the price. I always looked forward to those clinics and was pleased that the coaches were interested.

My First Clinic

The first clinic I put on was with Dick Green and Sal Domingues of Tucson, Arizona. It was held in a prison in Safford, Arizona and like at San Quentin, there was a lot of talent but not much in style. As always these prisoners had good athletic coordination as most of them had done successfully gymnastics and wrestling. Sal was a national record holder and Dick was a national coach. They helped immensely.

Three of the lifters progressed to become national champions. Two made so much progress they qualified and went to the North American

Championships held in Montreal, Canada. Taking inmates out of prison if for only a few days was a big ordeal as would be expected. But it all worked out well as I mentioned earlier. The national board of directors had a lot of reservations but when it worked so well it opened the door for further such successful trips. You can imagine how worried the national directors were. Bob Crist was the chairman at that time and many innovations were done under his leadership.

Traveling across the country was also a success. I did this for sixteen years.

I constantly kept in touch with the leaders in the field from the USA to South American to Central America to Asia to Europe. The big advances in the field were due to leverage changes and training changes, many of which I introduced.

Cortisol Testing

One of the things we had done when I was national Olympic weightlifting coach was blood tests before the camp, and after. We were interested to determine if we could see differences in cortisol levels. I had learned from the Polish that if one was training correctly cortisol would go up, and if training too much levels would go down. No matter how much a lifter over trained or undertrained it would show up. This is a valuable tool to accurately plan a lifter's training program.

Tearing Biceps While Spotting For Squatter

Spotting for a lifter doing squats can be dangerous. I was doing this with a lineman from the University of New Mexico in 1985. He had 408 pounds on the bar and was to do five reps. I said if he got stuck coming up I would pull up and he would continue to finish the squat. Well, he didn't and the bar fell into my hands and my biceps ripped out. Terribly, terribly painful and I fainted yelling as I fell. It took six months for the pain to subside. I could no longer do chins. With no biceps and not using my arms to pull, I actually became a better lifter by using my hips and legs more.

Many times the clinics led to other interesting adventures. One was when I had completed a clinic in the Los Angeles area during the Gulf War. The government had broadcast messages on the radio and TV warning people to keep their baggage secure so it would not be stolen. As I was leaving LAX, I was mugged by four men. I had opened the glass lobby door and set my baggage down to open the door when they tried to take my bags. As I held tight, they yelled and screamed and pounded my face and body. I yelled for help and some other passengers rescued me and the four men fled.

This was only 11:30 or noon. What took place after dark, I was told was much, much worse. I was really glad I was not taking a flight late at night! I was also told that the Los Angeles airport had incidences like this about once a month. My wife Sandra was very surprised to see me so bruised when I returned to Santa Fe. (I had gotten divorced from my first wife back in 1982 and Sandra and I were married in 1988.)

Al Vermeil

A word about Al Vermeil. Al was an excellent football player in high school and college and a very successful head football coach at a high school in Oakland. His brother, Dick, was head football coach of the Philadelphia Eagles. Al knew I was the National Weightlifting Coaching Coordinator and that I worked with the Dallas Cowboys in the summer. The Cowboys implemented lifting through their own strength coach and it worked out well. Al had heard that I used Olympic-style lifting with team training to help them run faster and hit harder so he told Dick Walsh, head coach of the San Francisco 49ers about it. Al then raised money and flew me in for a four day clinic to teach the Olympic lifts for the different positions. He felt that this would have the most benefit for his football team. The motions of this type of lifting were in contrast to the ones they were using for blocking, tackling, running, catching and throwing. I taught him and his players and in two years of using this type of training his team did so well that he was approached by Stanford to be their head strength coach and also approached by the San Francisco 49ers. He chose the 49ers job and wanted me to take the Stanford job. I couldn't do that at the time because I was running for the Santa Fe City Council. But we stayed in contact by phone and I went to San Francisco training camps frequently.

The 49ers really took to it and went from 3-13 to 8-8 to 13-3 and then won the Super Bowl. My first impression was I had never seen such big players run so fast. It just astonished me. The same discipline and thoughtful playing Al showed in his high school players worked with the 49ers. He showed a sense of authority and the players really respected that. At one time I noticed that one of the player's skills were sort of well, lackadaisical. I asked about him and Al said, "Don't worry. Walsh will have him eliminated before a week is out." And he was. That player had literally eliminated himself.

It was surprising to me that so many of the players didn't perform correctly when blocking or hitting an opponent the way many coaches I thought would have taught them. Al said that this is where the Olympic-style lifting will teach that, even with these pro players. And he was exactly correct. The feedback from the players was outstanding. They learned to do it quickly and effectively.

I spent two weeks there with Al and two weeks each of the following two years. With a coach like Al, this was fun. And Al got a lot of feedback not only from the players but the other coaches including Head Coach Bill Walsh. Al wanted everything to get better and better. I looked forward to our weekly phone calls.

Al had the drive to continually improve his coaching and he changed the thinking of the National Strength Coaches Association. I had spoken to that group before but I couldn't sell them on the importance of my training methods. Then Al spoke to the group and in one year had them change their minds. To give you an example, every NFL strength coach had their players bench pressing more and more and squatting at various depth, no matter the position they played. At one time in a talk to this group he asked why they used the bench so often. He then replied, "In bench pressing you are on your back, and when you are on back in our sport you're not making money." So true.

With Al's success with the 49ers he was asked by the National

Strength Coaches Association to give talks on Olympic-style as it pertains to football. The coaches used it and the word spread. Al could give a very convincing speech. So, in the end, with his teaching, out went bench presses and other static weight training. Al really had a way of getting his point across.

When Dick Vermeil accepted the head coaching position of St. Louis Rams, the Rams won the super bowl and Dick had Al come to the Ram training camps and put in Olympic-style lifting as their weight program.

Later, Al went to work for the Chicago Bulls basketball team as their strength coach. That was 1989 when the Bulls made the playoffs for the first time in years. He was there all during the 1990s when the Bulls had their best seasons. So every year from 1989 to 1999 Sandra and I went to the Bulls training camp in Chicago and helped Al perfect Olympic lifting. I was concerned about one thing so I asked Al about whether a certain coach would be back, and he said no. He was a divider, pitting one player against the other! But coach Phil Jackson united players. The most dramatic evidence was when the Bulls got Dennis Rodman from Detroit. Rodman had a reputation of being very individualistic. But Rodman became a team player for the Bulls.

Just to highlight the leadership Michael Jordan had when he played for the Bulls, there was one year when he didn't play basketball but played professional baseball, and the Bulls suffered without his leadership. Then when Jordan came back the next year, his leadership was there and the Bulls started winning again. He told me once that he wanted to give Chicago a world basketball championship and then if he could a world baseball championship.

Meanwhile, Al's coaching got better and better and better. Anybody who knows the psyche of a pro player knows that the coach had better be a mind coach as well as physical coach. The competitiveness of these superstars is just that—super! One early evening after practice Al, his wife Diane and Sandra and I were going to go out to dinner. Michael Jordan and Toni Kukoc from Yugoslavia were playing pool. When we came back they were still playing, not stopping until one beat the other. Now that's competition.

And speaking of Kukoc, one afternoon the players were coming in to get ready for practice and they started talking about how the day went. Many of them said it was a bad day—their kid's didn't do well in school, family problems, etc. Kukoc said, "Once in Belgrade when crossing the street I was being shot at. Now that is a bad day."

In his retirement Al and his wife Diane moved to Ohio to be close to his daughter, her husband and grandkids. He still gives clinics and I would highly recommend finding out where he will be and go to his clinic.

Santa Fe City Council, 1980–1984

During my last two years at Carlos Gilbert Elementary School, I served on the Santa Fe City Council as I mentioned earlier. During the time I was campaigning, since being bilingual was considered desirable, detractors would say, as they did when I was at Carlos Gilbert, "Yeah, he speaks Spanish but has a different accent." So I would simply say in my most friendly manner, "Well, your English has a different accent," and that usually shut them up.

At that time councilors were elected city wide. It took me three months to go door to door to as many homes as possible. People were usually very friendly. I can't say the same for their dogs. When there was only screen door to a house, one couldn't tell whether it was locked or not. If it wasn't the dogs really came at me, especially the German Sheppards. And they usually bit which meant a few trips to a doctor's office. Out of twenty-four bites, dog number eighteen was toxic.

One aspect of being on the City Council that created awkward situations was when people would ask for favors. They would usually say, "If we don't get favors we won't vote for you next time." I just had to learn to ignore those requests.

Before my first council meeting I asked five people I respected, who had been on the council or were then on the council, for advice. One bit of advice that was really important was when the council chambers were filled up with people, not to forget those who weren't in the chambers. Sometimes people who were in the chambers were very vocal and didn't always represent a good cross section of the feelings of the city at large. Another was for me to get to know my fellow councilors' backgrounds. Most were very upright. Others had very defined beliefs—not bad or good, just different. And it goes without saying that getting to know the mayor and city manager and others in the administration was desirable and this helped me do a better job in my council work.

I felt that I contributed two important things besides just the daily work. One was having funds for human services all in one place through a Community Foundation, and the other was expansion of the Valdez Industrial Park.

Having the whole of human services funding organized to work together was started elsewhere in the USA but died out during the depression. I found out that it was making a comeback in Oregon. So I went to Oregon and saw for myself how it started up again and was going quite well. In Santa Fe the various human services were always battling the city to get funding and the result was that nothing got done and there was lots of animosity created among the groups that needed funding. Santa Fe, like any city, had some hard core needs, like water and sewage and they couldn't spare the money. I was told that we would run into trouble with the Salvation Army, the United Way, and others, but I explained that was for different monies.

With problems like these sorted out the Community Foundation was ready to. We did need a lot of money to get it started. I approached Jimmy Rodgers to put on a benefit and we got the race track to loan Jimmy Rogers the track and get it underway. One Saturday night the race track was full, full. And people gave and pledged monies to the Community Foundation with its respected board of directors. That was decades ago and it keeps going, raising monies and funding the human resources. The community takes great pride in what it is doing.

One thing I noticed right away when I was starting on the council was that five of the eight councilors were on the finance committee. I didn't feel that this was good since financial decisions could be decided right in that committee without input from the rest of council members.

An outrageous action by one of the councilors once went like this. A big project was going in south of town. The vote on the council was close. This councilor at a council meeting and then even in the newspapers said, "Where is my money for my vote? They paid me to vote my approval!"

And once, on the council, the mayor tried to push through a project that I thought was suspicious. I argued about it. He got out of his chair, bent down to me and said, "You know how the game is played." I replied, "I don't know how your game is played, but mine isn't played that way." He told me to come into his office the next day. We went over this again and I brought in a tape recorder that had the whole conversation on tape. He then asked, "What do you want?" I said, "A fair vote based on fact." At a Christmas party, the guy who won the contract asked me how I knew the vote was wired. I said simply, "It didn't go out to bid."

We had a mayor during the time I was on the council who just couldn't say no. He nickel and dimed the city to death. I figured out what he was doing and on our last day of budget approval I vetoed $9 million off a $25 million budget. Most of the other councilors laughed but he got real angry. I compared the budget of Santa Fe and that of Las Cruces, very much the same in size and population. Our budget was eleven times that of Las Cruces. And they had a water system and transportation system which we didn't have. Going down line item by line item, they paid fewer employees more money than ours in Santa Fe. In the north here in New Mexico we are still influenced by the patron system where the head guy takes care of lot of employees at a lower wage. The school board did the same thing and our students rank lower. When will this change? A man from Atlanta once told me that the South didn't begin to change until more outsiders moved in. We live in a town where mediocrity is often the rule of thumb in my opinion. One didn't rise above one's neighbor or fellow employees or you are looked down on.

I had many experiences while on the council. A year into my first term a car ran me into an arroyo near my house. It was after a council meeting and I believe they were waiting for me. They said, "The mayor doesn't like the way you're voting." I told them that some of the mayor's policies were just not good for the city and that I had a right to object. That didn't go over at all and they dragged me out of my car and did a good job of kicking me around. But I defended myself fairly well without hurting them and they soon ran off.

Another time, going home from our gym I forgot that Alameda Street was a cruising street on Friday nights at that time. I turned onto it and two blond headed young men blocked my car, pulled my head down on the window, and hit me in the head and between the eyes. "This is our street," one of the young men said and I jumped out of the car and slammed one of them down against my car. That ended that. The very next week my eyes were still very black so I wore very dark sunglasses and never mentioned the incident.

During this time I also had concerns about the use of excessive force by the police department. I felt that the old saying, "let the punishment fit the crime," should be the rule of day because I had noticed what I thought was excessive force when it just wasn't necessary. So, on the council I introduced a bill along those lines. The voting on this took several months and was narrowly voted down. It was a very political vote with such matters as grandfathering some of the long standing police force and their practices in. But how much grandfathering? Never passed, but almost.

By and large I found members of the council and the mayor honest and well meaning. I didn't note any money changing hands but practices like annexing pieces of land outside the city when nobody was attuned to it happened. So infrastructure was put in. This annexed land was available so that some city councilors would buy it up. Then they would sell it at a good price. Another way of making money by councilors was to learn of a project taking place in the city and buy it up before anybody knew what had happened. I don't think I dreamed that up. Just saying.

Hispanic Militants and Lingering Effects

At one time Hispanic militants formed under the leadership of Reies Lopez Tijerina, an activist who led a struggle in the 1960s and 1970s to restore New Mexican land grants to the descendants of their Spanish colonial and Mexican owners. He became famous and infamous internationally for his 1967 armed raid on the Tierra Amarilla courthouse. He lived about one hour north of Santa Fe. He would roam around northern New Mexico spreading his message and this ended up scaring a lot of people. It seemed that he especially wanted to scare the Caucasians and he did.

I guess some of the militant attitude lingered on. For example, one Saturday I took my two young boys to a lake about eight miles north of Santa Fe. Our plans were to fish and hike the area. We parked next to this lake and before I could open the door about six men came up to the car on foot. They told me to drive on or they would harm my two boys. They got out their guns and fired in the air. It was their lake and wanted nobody else there. They were very serious and fired a couple of shots into the back of the car. I quickly drove away and never looked back.

I drove about an hour to Ghost Ranch which, a Presbyterian enclave. We were safe there and stayed the whole day before heading back to Santa Fe. The people were very kind and protective of us. Nearby was Abiquiu Lake. So not to have our trip amount to nothing, we drove down to it and there we fished and swam. A beautiful lake—clean and fun. It is formed by the Rio Grande River and at times water was let out for irrigation. It was like an oasis after our ordeal.

Metropolitan Water Board

Santa Fe has always had a water problem and after my council seat was up I ran for the Metropolitan Water Board. The chairman at that time was the owner of what was then called Bishops Lodge, a resort. And in that era a great place for Santa Feans and tourists to stay and enjoy their restaurant.

During my last two years on the council, my wife Sandra and I had opened up a gym (as I mentioned before with more on that later). I had taught the owners' two kids and felt right at home with him. His wife and two kids worked out at our gym. Both kids were interested in using weightlifting to better their running time and they did.

But he died and his wife had enormous responsibilities so we designed a gym for her and her clients at their resort. Before he died I felt together we had given the city council some great ideas, some of them specific.

Carl and Sandra's Gym

There were reasons for Sandra and I opening our gym. After years and years of coaching Olympic-style lifting, I did not want to go to the Olympic Training Camp and my days in the political arena were pretty much over. I thought having a gym of our own where I could train people

of all ages in Olympic-style weightlifting, strength and cardiovascular training, rehabilitation in other sports, and activities that improved their daily
lives would consolidate all I had learned. So with two physical therapists
we opened up a physical program in the Girl Scout Building with weights
and mats for rehab of injuries, programs for general conditioning, and
weight training to help athletes progress in their sports, and the physical
therapists had an exercise area.

But since we were all in the same large room, it wasn't long before
their client's yelling began to bother the lifters. The room was about
1,500 square feet in the bottom floor of the building. So we begin to think
about having a space just for our activities.

Meanwhile, my wife Sandra and I did all the teaching and coaching
at the gym. It made no difference whether you were an athlete or just
wanting to get in shape. We had a wide range of clients—from young boys
and girls to a 92 year old. We always stressed the concept that working
out at our gym should be fun. It was very successful and I really found
this work very satisfying.

After a few years there, and considering the space issue with noise,
Sandra and I moved closer to town and the gym got bigger—about 2,000
in the Sanbusco shopping center and we were their first tenants. We were
there five years until parking became a problem. We thought it best not
to have the physical therapists in the same organization and that's what
happened.

Then we had the opportunity to go to the De Vargas Mall where we
had about two times the space and plenty of parking. We put in a stairway
that one could use for exercise. And we put in a 35 yard track where we
could work on speed and use the wall for ball drills, both staying in one
place and moving. We also used weights for speed resistance training.
Using weights on the stairs and track added a lot to our training. Sandra
developed most of the exercises on the stairway and track. We had rings
put in, a climbing rope, a trampoline, and three stretching areas. We also
put in a dry sauna. We used the sauna to do warm ups. Also, alternating
sauna and cold shower helps take lactic acid out of the body that has
built up from the exercise. That way people wouldn't feel sore and would
recover quickly from the workout.

Because we had so much space we were now to ready to implement the Miller Plan of training outlined in my book, *The Miller Fitness Plan,* that I discuss in detail later. Basically a person does a hard cardiovascular exercise then stretches or goes to a non-cardiovascular activity, such as a stomach exercise. The cardiovascular exercise is usually a takeoff of one of the Olympic lifts either with dumbbells or barbells. After a circuit (three or four exercises) of this it is repeated two or three times. Very muscle building, fat burning. Stretch proof. We put in enough circuits that the workout lasts 45 minutes to over an hour, depending on the condition of the trainee. This plan gets the whole body involved and is done three times a week or at least two, because it is extremely efficient. On the other days clients do other activities and any other exercise game or sport. We really stressed fun and camaraderie at the gym. People said it was a home away from home. And the workout involves all systems of fitness and gives support to one's whole life

We offered all types of plans—general conditioning, rehab, sport specific, pregnancy, etc., for the elderly and the younger. And we did it well. Of the many pregnant women who have trained the whole nine months with us, many worked out up to two days before they delivered, some the day before. Sandra is a born teacher and the rest of our staff was excellent. And it is a joy to work with such a variety of people with such a variety of needs. It was a pleasure each day to go to work.

We used Olympic-style lifting as the basis. It is an athletic type motion and can be used in everyday life. Workout programs are individualized and change every six weeks and new goals set. Every goal is realistic. Why every six weeks? Because that is the time research and experience has proved to be practical.

The most important thing our clients were taught is that the hip, leg and upper body sequences of actions come into play in most everything we do. These actions are used in everyday life, physical activities, as well as high powered pro sports. Having learned these techniques, the injury rate and severity of injury is almost insignificant. Even our special needs people which include muscular dystrophy (MS), Parkinson's disease, cardiovascular referrals from medical doctors, improve faster than other people who don't use our methodology.

We have had doctors visit us and say that we bridge the gap between general physical therapy and Olympic caliber training for athletes.

We offered a service to many people who wanted to keep moving even though they were older or had sustained an injury.

Because we had clients who wanted to improve their performance through Olympic-style weightlifting, we got not only clients in traditional sports, but also clients in non-traditional sports. They brought their own needs, which would involve various adaptations of Olympic-style lifting. It has been a real educational experience devising programs for them. Different exercises were used including Olympic-style lifting and the variations of other training methods.

We got bull riders, horseback riders, and rowers (single and teams of four and eight). Police and firemen came too and gained in strength, power, flexibility, speed, and agility. These athletes are usually very precise and dedicated. Our other clients pick up a lot simply by training with them. When horse racing was going strong, our gym members really enjoyed watching these small riders lift so much weight.

It was one of our jobs to show how leverage plays so much in not only Olympic lifting but also in their specific activities in ways they never knew. After learning about leverage, they were able to put it to good use in their sport activity and also in Olympic lifting.

We did a lot of rehabilitation both with competing athletes as well as with people who had injuries and didn't want to give up their sports activities. They want to keep playing and not give up just because of an injury. We usually got a client after the physical therapist's treatment with their specific machines like ultrasound and electrical sensory therapy. If a rehabilitative client doesn't need such treatment from a therapist, we could take them right away as we knew our anatomy and leverages to do this the right way. Because we had used so many types of exercises, I believe we did a better job than the physical therapists in many cases. From time to time when medical people come in because they have heard of success we are having they are impressed.

I have said this before and I will say it again—we could help athletes get top performance through our system. Besides the dumbbells and barbells, we used the trampoline, rings, rope, parallel bars, four large stretching areas, use of wall balls, grippers, and skating slide, all which helped our clients advance even further.

When I was coaching the Russians, as I've said, they told me that to recover faster from a hard workout to alternate between hot two minute and cold fifteen second showers. Then repeat that four or five times. That worked. It apparently milks the lactic acid out of the body. I was also told that if one got an injury to put ice pack on for 25-35 minutes—not heat. Heat causes the injury to swell. Cold causes the injury to get smaller. Works great! We tell our clients to follow these guidelines and we have 100% success.

Sandra and I were in the gym six days a week and had built up many friendships among our clients over those many years.

A big satisfaction to me was to see so many people progress and to realize how long they had been coming to our gym. We had people who have been at the gym for thirty to thirty-five years. Many of our members have competed in Olympic weightlifting, winning in state and national meets. I have enjoyed being a part of their lives as the years progress. We have seen many marriages, long lives (our oldest at 102) and those that have started quite young, usually around eight years old. All those people who shared their ups and downs are a real blessing to us. And we have tried to be of great service to them.

I would like to point out some of these people by name and a little something about them. (Keep in mind that these facts were current at the time I wrote this book and I've mostly used the present tense in writing about them.)

John Stephenson

John Stephenson, now deceased, was over a hundred years of age when I wrote this book and came to us at the age of sixty-nine with a bad shoulder he got from swimming in a triathlon. His shoulder got much better and he really got into the sport of Olympic weightlifting, eventually being inducted into the United States Hall of Weightlifting Fame. He won ten national masters championships, three world masters champion-ships, eight national records, and four world records. He and his wife had a community farm where they grew vegetables, fruit trees and other crops, which they shared with the community. Driving home to Santa Fe from a worlds championship in Albuquerque, his car was totaled and his wife of 50 years killed. After that John would barely talk. He came back to the gym about three weeks after and just sat in the corner. Slowly, he started to lift again. He then went on to win three more championships.

Carol Wright

Carol Wright was nearing ninety at the time I wrote this book and she looked and acted like a middle aged person. She has won many ski championships and is still skiing. She has been at the gym since she was sixty-one and was able to avoid operations through shoulder and knee rehabilitations We have had many people avoid operations but Carol is the oldest.

Mike Hermanson

Mike Hermanson came to us in his late twenties and is now in his early forties. He is an accountant and has been head of the Kiwanis Club. The Kiwanis sponsor a big Labor Day event called Zozobra. Started in the late 1920s, it is a giant figure referred to as "Old Man Gloom." People come from the city, and all over the state and elsewhere and bring their dinners, sit on the grass and watch as Old Man Gloom is set afire. His burning down is a symbol of the old or troubling things going away so folks will have a fresh start. Mike has set many state weightlifting records and has placed in the top three at the national championships.

Luann C De Baca

LuAnn C de Baca was an aspiring national volleyball player and came to us to improve her ability in jumping and covering the floor with more speed. She started in her early thirties. She was named to a national women's volleyball team four times.

Carol Santandria

Carol Santandria is 4'9" and works at Los Alamos National Labs as a scientist. She won the national weightlifting championships and qualified for the worlds championships. She weighs 95 pounds and has snatched 62 kilos and clean and jerked 80 kilos.

Timmy Ortiz

Timmy Ortiz was national teen-age champion two times and set national records in both lifts.

Joaquin Chaves

Joaquin Chaves came to us as a senior at Santa Fe High school. He was a guard on the football team and injured his back. He recovered from the injury and won a national teen-age championship. He graduated from the University of New Mexico and is a strength coach there. And he has taken national weightlifting teams to world's championship.

Jerome Gonzales

Jerome Gonzales came to the gym at about the same time as Joaquin Chavez. Jerome won two national teenage championships and went on to become a successful engineer in Colorado.

Analysa Cohen

Analysa Cohen came to the gym about almost a decade ago and is now 88. I taught her kids in school. She came to the United States in 1942 from Denmark. She met her husband Saul there. She is a real inspiration to us and her fellow members. The spark, the energy and it keeps getting better.

Dick Lawrence

A group of former fighter pilots came to the gym and Dick Lawrence was one of them. His stories about flying across the Yalu River and shooting down migs in China are extremely interesting. His wife Bobbie joined him at the gym and both have since moved to Texas and are still working out. They are in their 80s.

Football And Basketball Players

Several football, basketball players have worked out to better themselves in their sports.

Joe Arellano

Joe Arellano has won national Olympic championships. Joe is a very successful contractor and specializes in roofs that last over fifty years. His wife Eilani also trains and is a very good Olympic lifter.

John Ruble and the Gym's "Book Table"

A former famous client of ours who passed away at age 95 inaugurated the gym's "book table" with a hundred plus books. Clients bring books in and take some home to read. This has been going on for over twenty years. Clients share what they are reading or have read. John had a PhD degree from MIT and Caltech and worked for large defense contractors. He was assistant Secretary of Defense under Robert McNamara. He could talk about anything in depth, write prize winning poetry, ski, and play tennis. We called him our Renaissance man.

Gene Hackman

Often we would have some well known clients. One morning I came in and one of our trainers told me that Gene Hackman was training with us. I asked, "Who's that?" She replied, "Haven't you ever heard of 'The French Connection'?" I said no. She stated that Gene Hackman was given an Academy Award for his acting in it. In time I got to know him.

Arnold Schwarzenegger

Arnold Schwarzenegger was in Santa Fe once shooting the movie "Twins." He was there for eight days and said he really liked the gym and its members. So he trained with the members. He said he felt like he was amongst brothers. His wife Marie Shriver trained there as did Danny DeVito's wife, star of "Cheers."

Joe Gutierrez

Joe Gutierrez took hundreds of pictures for the Air Force. When got out he went to work for the Camera Shop in downtown Santa Fe and did so for forty years. We had weightlifting as a mutual interest. He went from 205 pounds down to 160 and kept it off. He has successfully played racquetball, handball, and tennis. He is over 86 and still active in those activities and weight training. He is a great inspiration always doing his best, making others feel great.

Maria Benetiz

Maria Benetiz has been a national flamingo dancer for over forty years. She has trained at our gym on three different times. She has done all own choreography and has brought dancers over from Spain.

Lupe Martnez

Lupe Martinez has been a black belt in karate and an instructor at world champion games for years. He has had one leg amputated and he wants to keep his remaining leg and other parts of his body fit so he can continue his karate. He is a geologist and needs continued and increased strength to continue his profession which takes quite a bit of work in the open and low hill terrain. He is always setting physical goals for himself under our guidance. He is considered one of the best geologists in the southwest.

Jimmy Gonzales

Jimmy Gonzales, a contractor, lost both legs in a motorcycle accident right below the knees. He has rehabilitated so well that he is out in the field all the time. And he is a song writer who is reveling in that field and becoming recognized for his work.

Katie Chapyak

Katie Chapyak has come down from Los Alamos three times a week for seven years. She also has an amputated limb but has developed so much strength and balance that she can do anything she wants.

Sheila and Ed Heighway

Sheila and Ed Heighway are great Tango dancers and compete on a regular basis. The Tango is a very demanding dance and the training with us helps them get better and better.

Henry and Santonete Sadmeir

Henry and Santonete Sadmeir came to our gym for about fifteen years. He is from Germany and she from Switzerland. He started working out because he was getting to the point in handball that his hands hurt too much. Sandra takes him through his new programs because she Sandra speaks some German.

Zueleika

Zueleika dances all over the world doing dances that are part western and part mid-eastern. Her dances require much strength and endurance.

Sal Cristy

We had a Sal Cristy working out since he was eight. He is a pitcher and his father a policeman. He worked out with us until he went to Arizona State to College where he excelled as a pitcher.

Robert Bernstein, MD

Dr. Robert Bernstein is respected as one of the top endocrinologist in the state. He is an ardent outdoorsman who loves to spend days, even weeks in the outdoors. He trains in martial arts and regularly at our gym. He is a spoken advocate of regular exercise and proper nutrition.

Maria and Julia Lopez

Two sisters who have physical handicaps have been coming for years. Maria Cristiano Lopez has been able to get stronger and more efficient in her walking. In fact she recently returned from a walking trip of Spain, France and England. Her hip is deformed and when she came in she could barely walk. Her sister Julia has a deformed arm but has built strength and flexibility to do things with that arm that she couldn't before use.

Carmela Padilla

Carmela Padilla is an accomplished writer, having written books and articles on Spanish culture in New Mexico. One book, *Slow and Low,* is about the cars that have been lowered and attract attention when they go extra slow around the city, especially the plaza.

Andy Tyson

Andy Tyson was shot in the hip. His bone density was so terrific that the doctor said his working out saved his hip from being shattered.

Doris Carloson

Doris Carloson had minimal bone density and she is in her 60s. In one year of training with us her bone density is normal.

Al Grubesic

Al Grubesic's family came from Croatia and settled in New Mexico. His son John urged him to join the gym more than thirty years ago. He was elected to the Santa Fe city council and was always asked for his advice. He is well known in Santa Fe, having contributed much time, effort and money to the community schools and church. He was honored by the city as a Living Treasure for his outstanding contributions to the city.

I could go on and on but will stop here and say it is very rewarding to have adults who want to stay active work out year after year. Some have had bad injuries growing up but they want to stay active and have good health. Some people have very serious injuries and initially go to physical therapy. Then they come to us and I believe we often do a better job. My wife Sandra is an expert in nutritional counseling. Many people who come to her are confused because they read about magical diets in the news media. Sandra makes it simple, and clients really appreciate that.

After 34 successful years it is still going strong and we sold the business in January of 2016 to Joe and Eilani Arellano. At the time of the publication of this book, Sandra is still working there and I will again there when this book is published.

7

Writing Books

I wrote five books on Olympic-style weightlifting between 1972 and 2000 and they were a pleasure to write. Here they are along with the information on three books published by Sunstone Press:

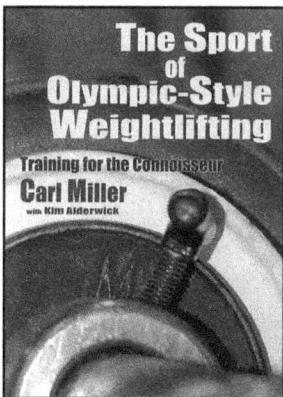

The Sport of Olympic-Style Weightlifting
Training for the Connoisseur
Sunstone Press
Price: $22.95 Softcover
ISBN: 978-0-86534-811-0

This book consolidates Carl Miller's extensive knowledge gained while pursuing his life's work in Olympic-style weightlifting. There are scientific principles behind Olympic-style weightlifting, and Miller's 50 years of lifting, researching and coaching provide valuable insight into the process of Olympic lifting. Whether you are an advanced lifter or a novice, Miller equips you with the tools to become a champion, even if it's in your own mind. For those lifters with the desire to compete, Carl's book will inspire you to immerse your body and mind in the intricacies required to be a winner.

Miller's success as a young weightlifter led him to a long and unique career coaching weightlifting, fitness and nutrition to elite athletes in the 1960s and 1970s, and later he spread his message about the benefits of weight training to a wider audience. As Coaching Coordinator for the U.S. Olympic weightlifting team, Miller put into practice many methods and techniques he gleaned from studying successful international lifting programs. The U.S. Olympic weightlifting team under head coach Tommy Kono won a record number of Olympic medals using assistant Olympic coach Carl Miller's coaching system. He gathered the best lifters in the country, had the best coaches in the sport, and introduced new lifting techniques to elevate the U.S. lifters to contenders.

Carl Miller has dedicated himself to analyzing and tweaking the techniques of Olympic lifting. During the 1970s, in addition to his duties with the Olympic team, he was a national coach, world coach, elementary school teacher and vice principal. As a teacher and vice principal Miller developed physical conditioning programs for the kids in his school. During his 30 years, and still counting, as founder and co-owner of Carl and Sandra's Physical Conditioning Center, lifters seek out Carl, his son Shane and staff for Olympic-style training. Carl and Sandra's Conditioning Center stands apart from other gyms because Carl Miller's philosophy revolved around the benefits of weight training long before it became popular. He weaves the hundreds of tiny components of Olympic-style weightlifting into beneficial fitness programs for gym members with a wide variety of profiles, and at the same time, his Conditioning Center trains a team of nationally competitive masters Olympic weightlifters.

The Sport of Olympic-Style Weightlifting provides the athlete with a comprehensive review of the critical elements that mold a champion. Winning isn't simply about lifting technique, eating the right food or visualizing lifts. You will discover the importance of body levers and the nuances of adjusting for your own unique body measurements, you will learn the finer points of planning the different phases of your training, you will be enthralled with the diverse programs available to incorporate in your routines, and you will grasp how your mind contributes to your accomplishments at critical points along your trajectory.

"Carl's honesty and integrity are demonstrated throughout this book as he provides precise instruction necessary to lift correctly, minimize injury and achieve optimal results. Carl has a unique collection of observations, statistics and facts gathered from nearly 50 years of coaching in the strength and conditioning world. He has coached at all levels of competition. I feel that this book is a must read for any serious student or coach interested in strength and conditioning."

    —R. Marvin Royster, MD, Orthopaedic Surgeon for Merrist School, Atlanta and the Atlanta Braves

"My friend Carl Miller has been practicing and coaching Olympic-style weightlifting at the highest level for 50 years. Few, if any, can match his knowledge and experience. When Carl speaks, serious lifters listen."

    —Clarence Bass, author of nine books on fitness and aging, including the most recent, *Great Expectations: Health Fitness Leanness without Suffering*, and a regular contributor to *Muscle and Fitness Magazine*

"*The Sport of Olympic-Style Weightlifting* is based on practical research and successful application by someone who has been in the trenches for many years. Carl has given some very insightful tips on training that not only apply to lifters but all athletes that I have trained over my coaching career."

    —Al Vermeil, Strength and Conditioning Coach for the Chicago Bulls, Chicago White Sox and San Francisco 49ers, and President, Vermeil Sports and Fitness, Inc.

"*The Sport of Olympic-Style Weightlifting: Training for the Connoisseur* updates Carl Miller's popular and quickly out-of-print *Olympic Lifting Training Manual* of the late 1970s. This new work reflects the best of Carl's teachings and is packed with tons of worthwhile tips and secrets to strength success. This book belongs on every weightlifting and strength coach's bookshelf."

    —Harvey Newton, author *Explosive Lifting for Sports*, USA Weightlifting National and Olympic Coach (1981-84), NSCA Executive Director (1995-99), Owner of Newton Sports.

The Miller Fitness Plan
Physical Training for Men and Women
Sunstone Press
Price: $22.95 Softcover
ISBN: 978-0-86534-481-5

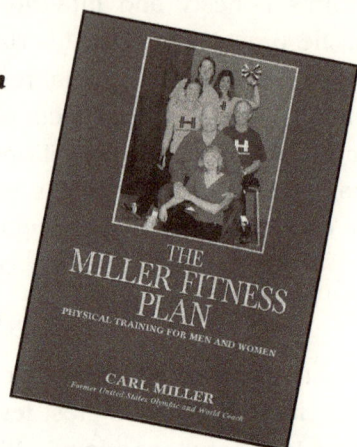

This readable, easy-to-follow guide to physical fitness incorporates Olympic coach Carl Miller's lifetime of experience. The book discusses the benefits of the motions used in Olympic-style weight lifting that contribute to strength, endurance and flexibility and Miller has fine-tuned his approach with decades of hands-on work with clients, both men and women, from age 9 to 90. The Miller Fitness Plan works for everyone, from athletes training for competition to reformed couch potatoes and people with physical challenges. Athletic weight training movements serve as a core for sound physical fitness, enabling people of all ages and abilities to see long term benefit, and have fun while exercising. Complete with photo illustrations, testimonials for those who have used the Miller Plan and advice on motivation, this book is a unique, user-friendly manual for getting and staying in shape that can be done at any gym or at home.

Carl Miller is the founder and co-owner, along with his wife, Sandra Thomas, of Carl and Sandra's Physical Conditioning Center which has been serving Santa Fe, New Mexico for more than 20 years. He has a master's degree in health, physical education and recreation with a specialty in exercise physiology, biomechanics and nutrition. He is a former United States Olympic and World Coach and the author of more than 50 articles and three books on Olympic-style weightlifting and athletic training. He has served as a consultant to many strength coaches in many sports, the most well-known of whom is Al Vermiel, former long-time strength coach for the Chicago Bulls basketball team, the San Francisco 49ers football team and the Chicago White Sox baseball team.

"Carl Miller, my lifelong friend, is the best there is at teaching athletic weight training to fitness-minded people in all walks of life. *The Miller Fitness Plan* works."

—Clarence Bass, author of the Ripped series, *Lean for Life* and *Challenge Yourself*

"Anyone interested in learning or instructing physical exercise should read Carl Miller's book. The step-by-step explanations in the pages here make clear the philosophy and principles that make the training program, as taught at Carl and Sandra's Conditioning Center, so productive and superior. I highly recommend *The Miller Fitness Plan* to all who wish to improve their physical condition for life."

—Tommy Kono, two-time Olympic champion, former Olympic coach and member, International Weightlifting Federation Hall of Fame

"I was very fortunate in my coaching career to have met Carl Miller. He was very willing to share his knowledge and ideas with me. I've used many of his concepts throughout my coaching career. In this book, Carl expresses his unique approach that will benefit anyone who truly wants to physically improve himself."

—Al Vermeil, strength and conditioning coach for the Chicago Bulls, Chicago White Sox and San Francisco 49'ers and president, Vermeil Sports and Fitness, Inc

"Few people know Olympic-style weightlifting better than Carl Miller. Fewer yet incorporate these exercises in the average person's fitness program. Get stronger, have fun and enjoy a new challenge. Follow *The Miller Physical Training Plan*."

—Harvey Newton, former national and Olympic coach and author, *Explosive Lifting for Sports*

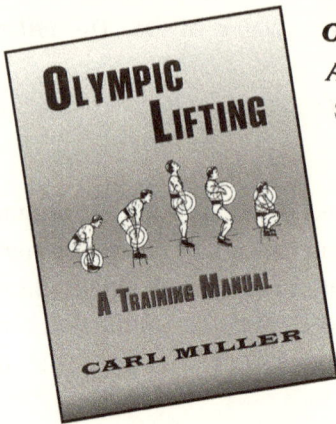

Olympic Lifting
A Training Manual
Sunstone Press
Price: $22.95 Softcover
ISBN: 978-1-63293-218-1

The information in this manual is primarily intended for Olympic-type lifters and coaches so they can improve performance in this sport. But since the hip and leg action of most other sports is similar to that of Olympic lifting, other sports participants and coaches will also find this manual useful.

Carl Miller is a former United States Olympic and World Coach and the author of more than fifty articles on Olympic-style weightlifting and athletic training. He has a master's degree in health, physical education and recreation specializing in exercise physiology, biomechanics and nutrition. He was the founder and co-owner, along with his wife, Sandra Thomas, of Carl and Sandra's Physical Conditioning Center in Santa Fe, New Mexico for more than twenty years and has dedicated himself to analyzing and tweaking the techniques of Olympic lifting. He is the author of *The Sport of Olympic Style Weightlifting* and *The Miller Fitness Plan*, both from Sunstone Press.

How to Teach Weightlifting in High School and College

This book is a great help to teachers, coaches in schools, and coaches in recreation centers. Every detail is covered to fit the needs of these instructors. For lifting to give the greatest benefit to sport Activities they must be neuromotor specific, first build strength, then power, and then endurance. Many years ago the programs only built strength and as a result athletes didn't get much benefit. That is why teachers and coaches didn't use weight training very much. Strength is the basis for power but power is not developed of there is no strength gained. Then the power comes from the added strength. Endurance can also can be increased with increased strength. But, again, gaining strength has to come first.

How to Use Weight Training for Your Specific Sport

This book is designed to help an athlete who uses mainly speed or mainly endurance.

When writing these five books it must be noted that they were written over many years, and besides our educational background we were always learning from our clients, trainers, and other coaches. They were developed and written in conjunction with our teaching and our experiences coaching people. They were a hands on approach that kept evolving and the books were updated throughout the years. We also gained valuable information as we read books from other countries and attended clinics in related fields. In addition to sport clinics we attended engineering, sport psychology, and medical clinics. We always used and innovated as we gained in experience and expertise.

For example, I thought about the methods I would present in *The Miller Fitness Plan* when I was getting a spinal fusion in Chicago. A former Mr. America and Olympic-style weightlifter Bob Gajda had written a series of articles in *Strength and Fitness.* These got me to thinking so during my recovery I went to the Duncan YMC in Chicago where Gajda and other top lifters trained. I talked with Gajda many times and he explained that to get the most out of weight training you had to have exercises that built muscle, cardiovascular health, along with fat loss. In addition to our daily talks I watched him work out. So I began to design programs based on the inclusion of all these aspects of physical fitness. This is known as circuit training, as I've mentioned earlier but bears repeating. Each circuit would start with a muscle building exercise that also burns fat and improves cardiovascular fitness. Then instead of resting, the next exercise would be a non-aerobic exercise, then a flexibility exercise. Usually the circuit has three or four exercises coupled with three or four circuits. The program would take 40-60 minutes and was designed that way. And the programs would last six weeks, the best time period for maximum benefit as I mentioned earlier in this book.

At the end of six weeks we would take measurements and compare them with those that we took at the beginning of the six week period. These measurements were weight, percent body fat, cardiovascular fitness, flexibly of ankle, back thigh, low back, chest force, upper back force, chest force, front and back force, and hip force.

We would set goals for each client because they all had different needs, and might have had different exercise training previously. Some had very specific needs such as muscle or flex problems. We had the client fill out a profile sheet which included exercise type, duration, medical problems, etc. And we would have a conference with their doctor if needed, as well as family input, and then set physical goals.

And my book, *Olympic Style Lifting* includes what I have called the Bulgarian method mostly since they had beaten the USSR at World Championships and Olympic Championships. They have very efficient training. While I have also used methods from all over the World and USA I have found that they were not as efficient in exercises and training and the utilization of the most beneficial training time.

Epilogue

I hope this book about my life has been both informative and entertaining. I've both learned and been entertained living it and the many events I've experiences have molded my interest in strength training and physical fitness and have given me a wonderful career path.

Many people might say I was ahead of my time. One thing I've learned in my life and long professional experience is this: the information one needs is, and has been, out there both in written form and in practical use. It just takes time to explore all the materials available. Practical use of what one learns is very important. Just reading or observing is okay and necessary but what one reads or sees must be thoroughly understood or appreciated and then put into practice to be of any use. I have found that if you can study just one area thoroughly what you learn will be transferred to some specific aspect of one's life. And this makes one more alive.

Garry Kasparov, former world chess champion of the former USSR thinks this way. I got a hint of this when his training coach came and participated in our camps during the two summers he came out to Santa Fe. If a person is really interested in an area, one will pull out ideas that are used in other areas of life.

I leave you with these 25 reasons why strength training is important:

1. Increases energy level
2. Improves fitness and overall health
3. Strengthens muscles, bones, joints and ligaments
5. Reduces stress
6. Improves confidence
7. Improves self-esteem
8. Improves mood
9. Fosters better sleep
10. Improves posture
11. Improves balance
12. Assists in endurance performance
13. Prevents injuries
14. Reduces healing time when injuries occur
15. Fosters independent living later in life
16. Makes everyday tasks easier
17. Improves sexual function
18. Creates muscle mass that fights diabetes
19. Prevents osteoporosis
20. Improves heart function
21. Lowers resting heart rate
22. Rectories bone density
23. Reduces depression and anxiety
24. Improves back pain
25. Improves function of the immune system

www.ingramcontent.com/pod-product-compliance
Lightning Source LLC
Chambersburg PA
CBHW021404090426
42742CB00009B/993